DELINQUENCY: SELECTED STUDIES

DELINQUENCY

Selected Studies

EDITED BY

THORSTEN SELLIN

AND

MARVIN E. WOLFGANG

University of Pennsylvania

JOHN WILEY & SONS, INC.

NEW YORK · LONDON · SYDNEY · TORONTO

Library of Congress Catalogue Card Number: 78-84961

SBN 471 77568 1

Printed in the United States of America

Contents

DELINQUENCY: SELECTED STUDIES

1

Measuring Delinquency

THORSTEN SELLIN AND MARVIN E. WOLFGANG

The chapters presented in this volume are by-products of a research which we, aided by the financial support of the Ford Foundation, began in 1960 and concluded in 1964 with the publication of its findings.[1] The purpose of that research was to examine the feasibility of constructing an index of delinquency that would, in contrast with traditional and entrenched methods in use, provide a more sensitive and meaningful measurement of the significance and the ebb and flow of the infractions of law attributable to juveniles, taking into account both the number of these violations and their character and degree of seriousness.

Official statistics of juvenile delinquency, currently published and generally assumed to provide a proper index to that phenomenon, seemed to us to be crude and quite inadequate for that purpose. They were either based on cases brought to court and, thus, ignored the high percentage of delinquencies—often as much as one half or two thirds—disposed of by the police by simple warnings or a referral to some social agency other than the court; or they were based on the number of juveniles charged by the police with specific crimes, the labels of which were supplied by the penal code and juvenile court statutes. We were convinced that police data on delinquency would furnish the best foundation for an index or indexes, but we were also convinced that the principles adopted by police agencies in compiling and publishing delinquency statistics were in need of reformulation. These principles had been followed by statistical services both here and abroad for generations. Therefore, it is no surprise that they were taken as guides in the preparation of, for instance, the statistics published by the Federal Bureau of Investigation in its *Uniform Crime Reports* which, in turn, became the model for reports issued by state and local police departments.

---

[1] Thorsten Sellin and Marvin E. Wolfgang, *The Measurement of Delinquency* (x, 423 pp., New York: John Wiley & Sons, Inc., 1964); *Constructing an Index of Delinquency. A Manual* (16 pp., Philadelphia: Center of Criminological Research, University of Pennsylvania, October 1963) .

CLASSIFICATION OF CRIME

Considering the large number of offenses defined by law—they may run into several hundreds in any given state, many of them varying only in minor details—it becomes necessary, for statistical analysis, to group them into relatively few homogeneous classes. The practice in the United States, as codified by the Committee on Uniform Crime Reports of the International Association of Chiefs of Police in 1930 and only slightly modified since then, is to group all offenses known to the police into twenty-six classes in a descending order from what is assumed to be the class containing the most serious crimes to the one with the least serious.

It is now a well-accepted doctrine that only certain kinds of offenses can be assumed to come to the knowledge of police agencies with sufficient regularity, so that changes in their number, when reduced to rates, would mirror changes in the total and partly unrecorded criminality involved. Therefore, the Standard Classification of Offenses (SCO) now in use separates the first seven offense classes from the rest and regards them as "index crimes." They comprise Part I of the SCO; the other nineteen classes fall into Part II. The "index crimes" are assumed to allow accurate statements about the rise or fall of these crimes *in toto* or separately. They are criminal homicide (exclusive of negligent manslaughter), forcible rape, robbery, aggravated assault, burglary, larceny of property valued at fifty dollars or more, and motor-vehicle theft.

It might seem reasonable to conclude that the process just described would produce a good index or indexes to crime. However, the principles of classification governing it cannot achieve that end in the most meaningful way.

First, one principle requires that if a criminal incident comprises more than one separately defined crime, such as the raping *and* killing of a victim, or the breaking into a house, stealing property therefrom *and* beating up the owner without inflicting serious harm on him, only the crime in each of these two events that has the highest place in the SCO hierarchy shall be counted, that is one homicide and one burglary; the other three offenses would be ignored.

Second, the classification of offenses according to the legal label attached to them ignores the fact that within each class there are great varieties that should not be equated. A robbery, for instance, may be the armed holdup of one or more persons, the infliction of serious harm to one or more victims, and the theft of thousands of dollars, or it may be the taking by a youngster of a few pennies from a younger child under threat of a beating. Between these two extremes there are numerous variants and combinations, all equated as robberies, regardless of the degree of injury to victims or the size of the property loss, as long as no one is killed or raped during the event. Should that happen, we would not learn of the robberies from the statistics at all; only the homicide or the rape would be counted. All the "index crimes" could be similarly illustrated.

Third, attempts to commit a crime are equated with completed crimes in most cases. Confounding attempts with completed crimes, rather than to provide a subclass of attempts under a given category of offenses, does not give a very clear picture of the crime situation.

Finally, every crime is given the same weight.

In summary, the use of the SCO, based on legal labels, suppresses all but the most serious crime, when the incident comprises two or more separate offenses and thus understates reality. By grouping together all offenses carrying the same legal labels, without taking into account differences characterizing them, the classification makes it impossible to observe possible qualitative changes in any given class of criminality over time. By not segregating attempted from completed crimes, the actual tangible physical harm to persons and property cannot be measured. The hierarchy of crimes in the classification does not guarantee that all offenses of a given class are necessarily more injurious than some of those placed in a lower class. Finally, whether a criminal homicide or a motor-vehicle theft, for instance, is counted, each is given the same weight of one.

It seemed to us that these defects, inherent in the SCO, would have to be overcome if a better idea were to be achieved. A different approach to the problem was evidently needed.

THE NEW APPROACH

Thanks to the Police Department of Philadelphia, Pennsylvania. we were given free access to the records of the department's Juvenile Aid Division, which deals with all offensive incidents involving juvenile actors. Each such event becomes the subject of an "offense report," which describes the event and its participants. A representative ten percent sample—1313 cases—of these reports for the year 1960 was drawn and subjected to intensive study. Two forms were designed, one for the event and one for each participant, and a variety of data from the offense reports were transcribed on these forms and coded for computer processing.[2]

---

[2] Copies of these form and full instructions for their use are found in our book, already cited, pp. 368-380.

As far as the event was concerned the most important information referred to when and at what address the event occurred; the age, sex, and race of the victim (s) ; the kind of place where the event happened; who discovered it, apprehended the offender, etc.; the number of offenders involved and whether or not they were turned over to the juvenile court; who prosecuted and who refused to prosecute; type of victimization; certain facts about property offenses, including the value of property lost or damaged; whether or not victims were intimidated and by what means; and the degree of injury inflicted on the victim (s) .

On the offender form, in addition to identification data, such as name, address, sex, age, race, and a number permitting the association of the offender with his offense, the most significant data referred to his disposition by the police; who apprehended him and under what circumstances; his relationship to the victim (s) ; and his prior record of police contacts.

The raw data on delinquency were thus made available. The next problem was what to do with them for the purpose of constructing an index. Here we had to make some crucial decisions. What should an index measure? Because the function of any index, be it a barometer, a cost-of-living index or a crime index, is to furnish an indicator that, as accurately as possible, permits the observation of the intensity of and the change occurring in a given phenomenon, a delinquency index should permit one to determine, both qualitatively and quantitatively, the intensity of delinquency and its change over time. Because juvenile delinquency is practically always identifiable as such only when an offender is apprehended and his age determined, our study had to be limited to delinquent events resulting in the apprehension of an offender. The unquestionably large number of delinquencies that never came to the attention of the police for some reason or other were beyond our reach. This brought up the matter of the reportability and detectability of juvenile offenses.

To shorten a long story, we concluded that since only certain kinds of delinquencies would most likely be brought to police attention with sufficient regularity, we could assume that the portion of such offenses thus made visible remained reasonably constant over time. Therefore, we decided that the index should be based on juvenile offensive events that caused actual physical harm to a victim and/or property loss or damage. We adopted the general idea underlying the SCO. All the offenses counted as "index crimes" in that classification were included in our index but, as will be seen later, our manner of dealing with such "index crimes" and our use, in addition, of some nonindex offenses in the SCO differ radically from current practice. We may have erred in referring to the index we ultimately developed as an "index of delinquency." It would have been more accurate to describe it as an index of juvenile offenses resulting in personal harm to victims or in the theft and damage to property, because all other forms of delinquency were excluded. In a sense, it became an index to the amount and degree of objectively measurable harm done by juveniles to the social norms protecting life and property in the community.

It will be recalled that the SCO separates its twenty-six offense classes by placing some in one section of the classification—Part 1—and calling them "index crimes" and the rest in a section called Part II. We also divided the 1313 events in our sample into two "classes," Class I containing the events on which our index was to be based. This class was subdivided into three groups. Subclass A included any event, *regardless of the legal title attached to it,* that produced bodily injury to some victim. In subclass B we placed events that produced no such injury but did involve the theft of property; in subclass C we included events that caused damage to property but did not involve either theft or personal injury. Our Class II contained seven mutually exclusive subclasses, none of which exhibited any of the features of the Class I events. Subclass D comprised events in which only the intimidation of someone was their characteristic; subclass E included attempts to steal something; subclass F, the victimization of a person; subclass G, the victimization of a commercial establishment, etc.; subclass H dealt with events where the community at large may be said to have been victimized; subclass I contained consensual offenses such as statutory rape; and subclass J, the juvenile status offenses, that is, acts punishable only when committed by juveniles, such as truancy, runaway, incorrigibility, etc.

Comparing our classification with the SCO, we found that of the 306 events on which we based our index, only 166 would have been listed among the "index crimes." This discrepancy was mostly due to the fact that our subclass A included physical injury due to simple assaults; subclass B, thefts of property valued under fifty dollars; and subclass C, property damage due to malicious mischief. None of these offense types was represented among the "index crimes" even though a large proportion of them in our subclasses A and C resulted in more serious injury to persons or damage to property than did some robberies, aggravated assaults, burglaries, or larcenies in the SCO.

No further reference will be made here to our Class II events, which played no role in the development of our index.

We noted earlier that by counting only the most serious component of a complex event, the SCO has failed to evaluate such events properly;

that by giving every offense a statistical value of one (1), adequate recognition has not been given to the relative seriousness of different offenses; and that this practice, regardless of the hierarchy of the classification, has not properly distinguished the varying degree of seriousness of offenses lumped together in any given category.

We tried to meet these criticisms by constructing an index that at least would not be subject to the same objections. By focusing on an event as a whole, whether simple or complex, we could take into account all its features. By our classification, which ignored legal labels, we could stress the tangible social harm produced by an event. However, the mere counting of events by a new method of classification would still give only a quantitative picture of delinquency. We needed, besides, some technique of estimating the relative gravity of the social harm caused by events in order to arrive at a qualitative measure of it. This required the dissecting of an event and giving to its components and aggravating features differential weights which, when summed, would give us a figure indicating the degree of harm involved.

Too much space would have to be given here were we to give a detailed description of the complicated process by which we attempted to solve this problem; we devoted to it four long chapters in *The Measurement of Delinquency*. Suffice it to say that we formulated 141 brief descriptions of events so constructed as to take into account characteristic features, such as its circumstance, the injury (if any) inflicted on a victim, intimidation and violence, value of property lost or damaged, etc. These events, as described, were rated on category and magnitude scales by about 750 university students, police line officers, juvenile aid police officers, and juvenile court judges. The judges lived in various counties of the state of Pennsylvania, the rest were from Philadelphia. The results of these attitude tests enabled us to give weights to various elements of an event and produce a form for scoring it. This is reproduced below.

We scored 504 events falling into the three subclasses of our Class I cases, but we decided to retain, for the construction of an index, only events which had at least a score of two, because we doubted that petty thefts or events in which someone needed little or no medical attention would be brought to the attention of the police with sufficient regularity. This decision resembles the one which excludes larcenies of values under 50 dollars and simple assaults from the "index crimes" of the SCO.

The scores of the 306 remaining events in our Class I were then reduced to rates, separately for the three subclasses and for all of them combined; these rates were indexes of delinquency according to our classification system. When we grouped them according to the SCO classi-

SCORE SHEET

Identification number (s) :_____

Effects of Event:　I　T　D　　(Circle one or more as required)

Elements Scored 1	Number × Weight 2　3	Total 4
I. Number of victims of bodily harm		
(a)　receiving minor injuries	1	
(b)　treated and discharged	4	
(c)　hospitalized	7	
(d)　killed	26	
II. Number of victims of forcible sex		
intercourse	10	
(a)　Number of such victims intimi-		
dated by weapon	2	
III. Intimidation (except II above)		
(a)　Physical or verbal only	2	
(b)　By weapon	4	
IV. Number of premises forcibly entered ...	1	
V. Number of motor vehicles stolen	2	
VI. Value of property stolen, damaged, or		
destroyed (in dollars)		
(a)　Under 10 dollars	1	
(b)　　10 - 250　...............	2	
(c)　　251 - 2000　...............	3	
(d)　2001 - 9000　...............	4	
(e)　9001 - 30,000	5	
(f)　30,001 - 80,000	6	
(g)　Over 80,000	7	

TOTAL SCORE　_____

fication in use and computed weighted rates per 10,000 juvenile population in Philadelphia, 7 to 17 years of age, we found that the SCO rate for "index crimes" against the person (homicide, forcible rape, and aggravated assault) was 68.95, while our rate for events involving personal injury was 135.28. Corresponding rates for property offenses were 115.7 and 156.3, respectively.

That our scoring system produces an index different from the one based on SCO is therefore obvious. The important question is whether our system is superior for measuring harm to persons and property by illegal acts. The answer can only be derived from an examination of the principles of classification and estimation on which the two indexes are based. If the criticisms we have made of these principles as applied by the SCO are acknowledged to be justified and if the principles we have followed are not subject to the same criticisms, our system would appear more defensible. Furthermore, it can be applied to crime in general, since it was found that the age of the offender did not affect the degree of seriousness attributed to the events scored by the raters.

At least two objections to the use of our system might be made by police, judicial or correctional agencies, even if they were to acknowledge its value. One would be that operating it would add to the cost of administration. This is not a serious objection, for with proper management the cost would be minimal. The second objection might be that by eliminating legal labels, traditional information highly thought of by administrators and people in general would be lost from statistical reports. This objection could be met, for instance, using our Class I events of personal injury to some victim as an example, by further subdividing this class according to the legal titles of the offenses involved in the events, be they simple or complex.

Because our research was limited to one metropolis, the question might also be raised that its scale values for the components of events and their aggravating factors would not be applicable elsewhere. It is interesting to note, however, that several replications of our research have been made or are under way in the United States and abroad and that a suprising agreement with its results has been found.[3] Although we have

---

[3] Since publication of *The Measurement of Delinquency* there have appeared several replications of the scaling process or researches that have used the scale scores derived from the Philadelphia population. The most elaborate replication has been made in Canada under support from the Canadian Research Council. This work is described in detail by Dogan Akman and André Normandeau, "Towards the Measurement of Criminality in Canada: A Replication Study," *Acta Criminologica* 1, 135-260 (January 1968). See also by the same authors, *Manual for Constructing a Crime and Delinquency Index in Canada* Montreal: University of Montreal, 1966; "The Measurement of Crime and Delinquency in Canada," *British Journal of Criminology* 7, 129-149 (April 1967). Also D. Akman, A. Normandeau, Stanley Turner, "Replication of a Delinquency and Crime Index in French Canada," *Canadian Journal of Correction* 8, 1-19 (January 1966); Aron Walker, "Replication of Philadelphia-Montreal Scaling of Seriousness of Offenses," Harvard University (typescript), n.d. Akman and Normandeau have also executed a replication study among university students and blue-collar workers in England, and Guy Houchon and A. de Boeck plan the publication of a replication in the Congo.

suggested that the application of our principles of scaling and classification in studies in other states and countries should be based on independent attitude tests, it is gratifying to know that, on the whole, the scale we devised appears to be generally useful.

Because the problem we had set out to study compelled us to focus on delinquent events, our sample was one of such events and not one of juvenile delinquents. We did collect certain data about the participants in delinquency and in our report we utilized some of these data, but we had to bypass a great many interesting problems, which would have required more extensive study of the delinquents. A few of them are dealt with in this volume of essays. Their authors were all graduate students at the University of Pennsylvania and participated in the original research in one way or another, one as a research associate (S. Turner), two as research fellows (B. Cohen, W. H. Hohenstein), and one as a volunteer (A. Normandeau). The three last mentioned possess master-of-arts degrees in criminology and, in 1968, Cohen and Normandeau received doctorates in sociology. Turner is now teaching in the sociology department of Temple University, Philadelphia, and has completed his studies

---

Additional replication studies of the psychophysical scaling are in process in New Jersey by Robert Figlio, among inmates of correctional institutions; by Angel Velez-Diaz, under supervision by Edwin Megargee, at the University of Puerto Rico; by Dusan Cotic in Yugoslavia; by Menachim Amir in Israel; by Herman Roether with sex offenders on probation at the Philadelphia General Hospital; by the state of California in an announced research project, and by the National Opinion Research Center, University of Chicago. Other studies in process that are known to have used the scale scores for judging success of demonstration or action programs have occurred in Boston, in Kentucky, and in New Jersey. In a further analysis of the Glueck Prediction Table relative to recidivism, the New York City Youth Board used the scale scores. See Maude M. Craig and Laila Budd, "The Juvenile Offenders: Recidivism and Companions," *Crime and Delinquency* 13, 344-355 (April 1967). In a study of hidden delinquency, Martin Gold found utility in the scale scores; see Martin Gold, "Undetected Delinquent Behavior," *Journal of Research in Crime and Delinquency* 13, 27-46 (January 1966). The *Social Progress Report* (forthcoming) of the Panel on Social Indicators of the Department of Health, Education and Welfare is planned with use of the scale scores in the chapter on "Public Safety," under the supervision of Mancur Olson.

Several papers have discussed the methodology of the scaling of crimes by this process. Included among these are S. S. Stevens, "A Metric for the Social Consensus," *Science* 151, 530-541 (February 4, 1966); S. S. Stevens, "On the Operation Known as Judgment," *American Scientist* 54, 385-401 (December 1966); G. N. G. Rose, "Concerning the Measurement of Delinquency," *British Journal of Criminology* 6, 414-421 (October 1966); D. Akman, Robert Figlio, A. Normandeau, "Concerning the Measurement of Delinquency—A Rejoinder and Beyond," *British Journal of Criminology* 7, 442-449 (October 1967). Relative to the utility of the scale scores in crime statistics in general, see Leslie T. Wilkins, "New Thinking in Criminal Statistics," *Journal of Criminal Law, Criminology and Police Science* 56, 277-284 (September 1965).

toward a doctorate at that institution. Hohenstein is instructor of sociology at Princeton University, and Cohen and Normandeau are assistant professors at Queens College, New York City, and the University of Montreal, respectively.

2

Delinquency and Distance

STANLEY TURNER

A number of interesting questions arise when one considers the matter of the relationship between the place where a delinquent lives and the place where he commits his violation of the law. How far does the delinquent live from where his offense takes place? Does the type of his offense affect that distance? And finally, does the presence of an accomplice have any effect on this relationship? It would also be interesting to compare the replies to these questions with findings of studies of distance involving adult offenders and their offenses and with studies where distance has been examined in relation to the selection of marriage partners, migration, removals, etc. This article will focus on all of these matters, using information available for certain types of delinquent events included in the research reported by Sellin and Wolfgang in their book, *The Measurement of Delinquency*. The events chosen were those in which offenses resulted in bodily injury to victims and/or the loss or damage to property; they represented a ten percent sample of delinquent events known to the police of Philadelphia in 1960. We shall refer to these events as index events because they were the ones which furnished the basis for the index of delinquency contributed by the authors mentioned.

The first question considered was: how far away does the offender live from the scene of his offense? To answer this question the location of each offense was pinpointed on a map of Philadelphia approximately ten feet long; then the residence of each offender was plotted and the "taxicab" distance from the offense to the residence was measured by using a map measure (watch pattern). Index events were selected because:

Index offenses have a "real location", that is, they occur at an obvious location. Many nonindex offenses have a vague location; truancy, possession of burglary tools, runaway, intoxication, incorrigibility, for instance, all have a diffuse or continuous location. Index offenses involve physical injury, theft, or property damage and can almost always be pinpointed.[1]

---

[1] Some exceptions can occur. For instance, police may discover a juvenile riding a bike which the offender admits that he stole but will not disclose the place from which he stole it.

Index offenses were selected as more reliable indicators of changes in the extent of delinquency. It was felt that using them would present a more stable picture of the relation between delinquency and distance.

Certain alternative ways of measuring distance exist but were rejected.

1. Measuring the distance from where the offense occurred to some fixed point such as the center of the city.[2]

2. Measuring the distance from the offender's residence to the victim's residence.

3. Measuring the distance from the offense to the victim's residence.[3]

Method 1 was rejected since it assumes a point that is somewhat arbitrary (the "center" of the city, for instance) or has no relevance to the offender. Whatever influences the distances that offenders go, it is not a matter of distance from a common fixed point.

Methods 2 and 3 are of use only when the victim and the offender meet, as in homicide. But in most index crimes this is not true. Or in some crimes there is no specific victim at a specific residence. Damage to city property, embezzlement in a large corporation, etc., would all be index crimes, but with no specific residence for the victim.

Similarly, there are various methods of measuring the distance from the offense to the residence of the offender.

1. Measure the beeline distance from the offense to the offender's residence.

2. Measure the distance from the center of the census tract of occurrence to the center of the census tract of residence.

The first method understates the true distance by a roughly calculable amount. The second method introduces a more complicated bias. Any offense occurring in the same census tract of residence is given a distance of zero; thus, whether an offense gets assigned a score of zero depends in part on how far the offender travels and how large the census tract is. Furthermore, the size of a census tract is inversely related to its population.

For these reasons we decided to use the more arduous method of taking the minimal estimated route from the offense to the offender's residence. Distance was read off the measuring wheel to the nearest unit and transcribed onto a card with certain other information.

---

[2] R. Clyde White, "The Relation of Felonies to Environmental Factors in Indianapolis," *Social Forces*, 10 (4), 498-509.

[3] Henry Allen Bullock, "Urban Homicide in Theory and Fact," *Journal of Criminal Law, Criminology and Police Science*, 45, 565-575, (January-February 1955).

REMOVAL OF BIAS FROM THE DATA

Two biases were detected in the data: first, the sample was a ten percent systematic sample of offenses and in every offense that was selected, all offenders were used. This means that the sample was a cluster sample of offenders, not a systematic sample. The residence of one offender is correlated with the residence of the other offenders in the offense: if one offender is so many units away from the offense, all are. For this reason, the decision was made to use the average distance of all offenders in an offense. Thus, one and only one distance figure was used for each offense: the arithmetic mean of all offenders participating in the offense.

The second bias was introduced by the device used to measure distance. The map measure is a device that looks like a pocket watch with a small wheel at the bottom. The wheel skims along the surface of the map and causes three hands under its glass face to turn. These three hands measure inches, feet, and tens of feet. The raw data obtained from this wheel displayed heaping at multiples of two. This was probably due to the tendency to round numbers off to the nearest even digit. To eliminate this bias, we gathered the data into groups five units in size. Thus, instead of having units of length equal to 125 feet, we presented the data in units of 615 feet (5 times 123). The raw data appear in Fig. 1. The same data are presented but, instead, the cumulated percentage of cases as a function of distance is presented in Fig 2. These figures show that the median

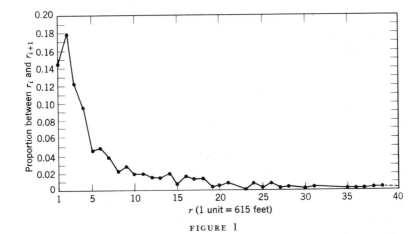

FIGURE 1

Proportion of index offenses occurring between r_i and r_{i+1} (distance between place of residence and place of occurrence in units of 615 feet). Last 5 percent of cases not graphed. Farthest value = 198 units.

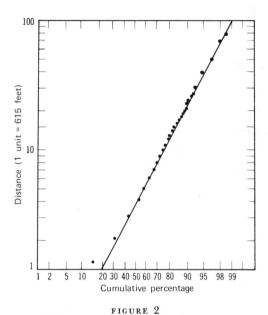

The cumulative percentage of index offenses occurring at a given distance (values plotted on log-normal paper).

distance traveled was 3.5 units (about 40% of a mile), three quarters of the offenses took place within one mile, and the range was from zero units to 23 miles (198 units). Two main facts stand out.

1. Most offenders live a short distance from their offenses.
2. The proportion wanes with distance.

DISCUSSION

The data thus far presented overlook one fact. As the distance increases, larger and larger amounts of area are included. Thus, going out one unit of distance from a point includes all the area swept out by a radius one unit in length; but going out two units from the same point sweeps out much more than twice as much area. This implies that one should divide the proportion of events that take place so many units from a point by the area included. That is,

$$Y_i = \frac{\sum_i P(r_i)}{\pi r_i^2}$$

Where P (r_i) = the proportion of cases in a circle r units in radius and Y_i is the cumulative proportion of events per unit area.[4] The data are presented in Table 1.

TABLE 1
Frequency and Distance

r	f	cum f	P	cum P	cum $P \over \pi r^2$
1.1	73	73	.145	.145	.0383
2.1	90	163	.179	.325	.0234
3.1	62	225	.123	.448	.0148
4.1	49	274	.098	.546	.0103
5.1	24	298	.048	.594	.00726
6.1	25	323	.050	.643	.00550
7.1	20	343	.040	.683	.00431
8.1	12	355	.024	.707	.00343
9.1	14	369	.028	.735	.00282
10.1	10	397	.020	.755	.00236
11.1	10	389	.020	.775	.00200
12.1	8	397	.016	.791	.00172
13.1	8	405	.016	.806	.00150
14.1	10	415	.020	.827	.00132
15.1	4	419	.008	.835	.00116
16.1	8	427	.016	.851	.00104
17.1	7	434	.014	.864	.000941
18.1	7	441	.014	.878	.000854
19.1	2	443	.004	.882	.000770
20.1	3	446	.006	.888	.000700
21.1	4	450	.008	.896	.000641
22.1	1	451	.002	.898	.000536
23.1	4	455	.008	.906	.000497
24.1	2	457	.004	.910	.000460
26.1	4	461	.008	.918	.000429
27.1	2	463	.004	.922	.000400

[4] Another and perhaps better way of presenting these data would be to divide r into a number of nonoverlapping intervals such that a significant number of events occur in each interval. Divide the number of events in the interval by the area relevant to the interval. Thus, if Δr_i is a band and r is the midpoint of Δr then $2\pi r \Delta r$ is the width of the band. Y_i in this case would relate to the probability per unit area and be plotted against r. This way would have the property of additivity, that is, the probability of an event falling in either of two areas would be the sum of their respective probabilities.

TABLE 1   *Frequency and Distance*—Continued

r	f	cum f	P	cum P	cum P / πr^2
28.1	2	465	.004	.926	.000373
29.1	1	466	.002	.928	.000326
31.1	2	468	.004	.932	.00307
35.1	1	469	.002	.934	.000241
36.1	1	470	.002	.936	.000229
37.1	1	471	.002	.938	.000217
38.1	2	473	.004	.942	.00207
39.1	2	475	.004	.946	.00197
40.1	1	476	.002	.948	.000188
41.1	2	478	.004	.952	.000179
43.1	1	479	.002	.954	.000164
45.1	1	480	.002	.956	.000150
46.1	1	481	.002	.958	.000144
47.1	1	482	.002	.960	.000138
48.1	2	484	.004	.964	.000133
49.1	1	485	.002	.966	.000128
50.1	1	486	.002	.968	.000123
53.1	1	487	.002	.970	.000110
54.1	1	488	.002	.973	.000106
58.1	1	489	.002	.974	.0000919
63.1	1	490	.002	.976	.0000780
70.1	1	491	.002	.978	.0000634
74.1	1	492	.002	.980	.0000568
76.1	1	493	.002	.982	.0000540
77.1	1	494	.002	.984	.0000527
79.1	1	495	.002	.986	.0000502
84.1	1	496	.002	.988	.0000445
98.1	1	497	.002	.990	.0000327
99.1	1	498	.002	.992	.0000322
133.1	1	499	.002	.994	.0000179
138.1	1	500	.002	.996	.0000166
146.1	1	501	.002	.998	.0000148
198.1	1	502	.002	1.000	.00000811
Total		502	1.000	1.000	

An analysis of Table 1 shows that the relation between the cumulative proportion of index offenses per unit area and distance is almost linear except for distances a very short way from the offender's residence. This can be corrected by plotting the offenses not against r but against $r + k$ units of distance. In this case, k is estimated by trial and error at roughly two units. Thus the cumulative proportion of events per unit is plotted not against r but against $r + 2$. The results of these corrections are shown in Fig. 3. Here the plot is essentially linear on log-log paper. The interpretation of k is similar to the threshold in psychological experimentation. The offender tends to commit offenses nearer to his residence, and his tendency wanes as distance increases. However, very close to his residence, say a block or two, he is less likely to commit as many offenses as we would expect. Some additional comment on this will follow.

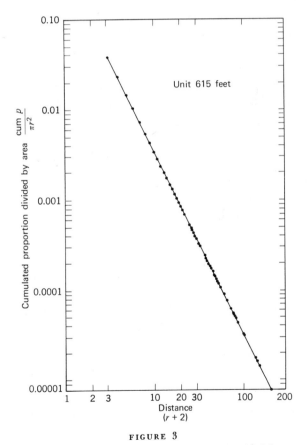

FIGURE 3

Cumulated proportion of index offenses at a given distance divided by area and plotted against that distance plus 2 units.

INTERNAL COMPARISONS

The data were broken down and plotted separately in two ways.

1. Offender was alone versus offender having one or more accomplices.

2. The offenses involved bodily injury or, lacking bodily injury, involved property theft or, lacking both injury and theft, involved property damage; all index offenses must have at least one of these features.

Table 2 shows the results of this procedure and the same data are plotted in Fig. 4.

There is little difference among any of the groups plotted except that the size of the constant added to the independent variable is larger in some cases than in others. Figure 5 may clarify this.

Figure 5 illustrates one possible interpretation: in many crimes the offender runs some risk of identification. In fact, in crimes against the person the victim is frequently known to the juvenile. The largest additive constant is in the offense lacking physical injury but involving theft. In these cases the offender goes somewhat farther away than in others, perhaps in order to find a victim unknown to him. Additionally, in some cases, what the offender steals may be identifiable. Large items such as bicycles and autos seem to fall into this category. If the offender intends to steal a bicycle and use it himself, a wise rule would be to steal it outside the radius in which he intends to use it.

When the offender is accompanied by an accomplice, they both tend to live near each other. If the above reasoning about the threshold of distance is true, then when they are together the threshold should be somewhat greater than in the case of a single offender. This is illustrated in the second case in Fig. 5.

COMPARISONS WITH OTHER STUDIES

In order to compare the present study to other forms of distance studies so as to find out if distance and criminality might differ from distance and other social events, data were taken largely from an article by Gunnar Boalt and Carl-Gunnar Janson.[5]

The results of plotting these studies are shown in Fig. 6 and Tables 3, 4, and 5.

---

[5] "Distance and Social Relations," *Acta Sociologica*, Vol. 2, Fasc. 2, pp. 73-97, 1957.

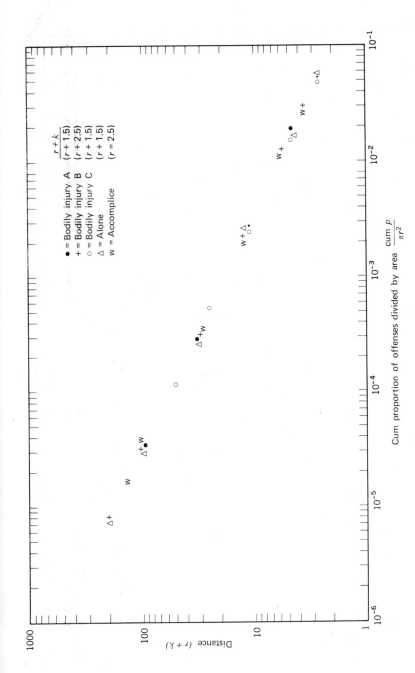

FIGURE 4

Cumulative proportion of offenses at given distances by offense type and by presence or absence of accomplices.

TABLE 2

Partial Table of Cumulative Proportion of Offenses at a Given Distance by Offense Type and by Offender Alone or Offender with Accomplice(s)

Bodily Injury Offenses					Alone			
r	cum f	cum P	$\dfrac{\text{cum } P}{r^2}$		r	cum f	cum P	$\dfrac{\text{cum } P}{r^2}$
1.1	229	.200	.0526		1.1	49	.184	.0485
3.1	81	.559	.0185		3.1	138	.519	.0172
10.1	119	.821	.0026		10.1	213	.801	.00250
31.1	137	.945	.000311		31.1	250	.940	.000309
98.1	145	1.000	.0000331		99.1	263	.989	.0000320
					198.1	266	1.000	.00000811

Thefts					Accomplice			
r	cum f	cum P	$\dfrac{\text{cum } P}{r^2}$		r	cum f	cum P	$\dfrac{\text{cum } P}{r^2}$
1.1	31	.108	.0285		1.1	24	.102	.0268
3.1	110	.385	.0127		3.1	87	.369	.0122
10.1	201	.704	.00219		10.1	166	.704	.00219
30.1	260	.909	.000319		30.1	218	.924	.000325
98.1	282	.986	.0000326		98.1	235	.996	.0000329
198.1	286	1.000	.00000811		138.1	236	1.000	.0000167

Damage					All Offenses			
r	cum f	cum P	$\dfrac{\text{cum } P}{r^2}$		r	cum f	cum P	$\dfrac{\text{cum } P}{r^2}$
1.1	13	.183	.0482		1.1	73	.145	.0383
3.1	34	.479	.0159		3.1	225	.449	.0148
10.1	59	.831	.00259		10.1	379	.755	.00236
24.1	70	.986	.000540		20.1	466	.928	.000326
53.1	71	1.000	.000113		98.1	497	.990	.0000327
					198.1	502	1.000	.00000811

These studies show a good deal of similarity to the present study when presented in the form used. In fact, what may be the explanation is the geometry of the situation rather than the sociology.

We propose that the general equation describing distance and de-

Offender Alone

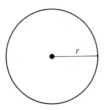

Rule: Go out from residence a distance *r* to avoid identification.

Offender with Accomplices

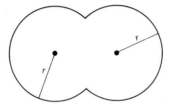

Rule: Same

Offender Steals a Vehicle

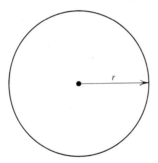

Rule: Go out from residence a distance *r* which is greater
than the distance in which you intend to use the vehicle.

FIGURE 5

linquency (and a number of other social events as well) is a power function of distance with a negative exponent. That is

$$Yi = a\,(r_i + k)^{-b}$$

where Y_i is the cumulated proportion of events per unit area, a is a scale

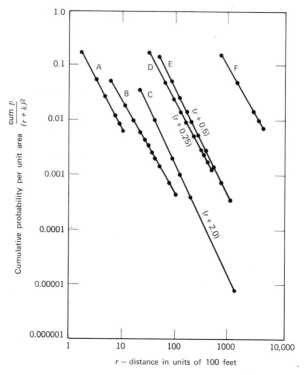

Key	Study	Distance between	Place	Date	N	Unit
A	Dodd	Tellers and hearers of a slogan	C — ville	WW II	125	50 Yds
B	Bossard	Pairs of marriage license applicants	Philadelphia	1951	5000	1 block
C	Present	Delinquents residence and offense location	Philadelphia	1960	502	615 ft
D	Bullock	Residence of murderer and offense location	Houston	1945 – 9	489	0.5 mile
E	Stouffer	Removals from 12 census tracts	Cleveland	1933 – 5	12,292	3000 ft
F	Bergsten	City of residence, and birthplace	Vä x jö	1940	15,609	20 lm

FIGURE 6

Cumulative probability of events per unit area plotted against distance for various studies.

factor relating to the unit of measure of distance, r is the distance, k is a constant estimated from the data and is very small with respect to the range of r. In our present study, the values for all cases combined are

$$Y_i = 0.33 \ (r_i + 2)^{-2}$$

and **Fig.** 7 shows how well the data points fit the above equation.

TABLE 3

Frequency and Cumulative Probabilities per Unit Area of Various Events

Stouffer (Unit 3000 ft)			Bergsten (Unit 20 km)			Dodd (Unit 50 yards)		
r	f	$\dfrac{\text{cum } P}{r^2}$	r	f	$\dfrac{\text{cum } P}{r^2}$	r	f	$\dfrac{\text{cum } P}{r^2}$
1	5,585	.145	1	8,870	.181	1	67	.171
2	2,471	.0521	2	1,730	.0540	2	23	.0573
3	1,313	.0269	3	1,064	.0264	3	12	.0289
4	737	.0164	4	470	.0155	4	10	.0178
5	431	.0109	5	717	.0105	5	4	.01188
7	537	.00585	6	347	.00748	6	5	.00856
10	475	.00299				7	4	.00650
15	532	.00139						
20	174	.000793		15,609			125	
31	37	.000331						
	12,292							

Removals in Cleveland, Ohio, from 1933-1935, for Whites in 12 census tracts.

Cited in Boalt and C. Janson, *op. cit.*

Distance from residence (Växjö, Sweden) to birthplace.

Bergsten: Sydsvenske Födelseortsfält (birthplace areas in southern Sweden), Lund 1951, *op. cit.*, pp. 65-66.

Cited in *Distance and Social Relations*, G. Boalt and C. Janson, pp. 73-97.

Dodd, S. C., "Testing Message Diffusion in Controlled Experiments: Charting the Distance and Time Factors in the Interactance Hypothesis," *Amer. Soc. Review*, 18, 410-416, (1953).

Distance between tellers and hearers place of residence for 125 pairs of persons in "c-ville."

TABLE 4

Bossard Unit = 1 Block (500 Feet)

	1885-1886		1905		1915		1951	
r	f	cum P / r^2	f	cum P / r^2	f	cum P / r^2	f	cum P / r^2
1	1063	.0677	220	.0141	373	.0237	859	.547
2	264	.0211	239	.00730	201	.00914	304	.185
3	187	.0107	264	.00511	207	.00552	210	.00971
4	178	.00673	230	.00379	226	.00401	155	.00608
5	196	.00481	180	.00288	176	.00301	151	.00428
6	187	.00367	190	.00234	175	.00240	119	.00336
7	147	.00288	190	.00196	163	.00198	91	.00258
8	139	.00235	137	.00164	130	.00164	80	.00206
9	134	.00196	128	.00140	120	.00139	68	.00168
10	117	.00166	142	.00122	124	.00121	79	.00141
15	463	.000870	469	.000676	396	.000649	284	.000707
20	290	.000536	321	.000431	279	.000409	197	.000429
$N =$	5000		5000		5000		5000	

[a] Distance between residences of first 5000 pairs of persons obtaining marriage licenses in Philadelphia 1885-86, 1905, 1915, and 1951.

[b] J. H. S. Bossard, "Residential Propinquity as a Factor in Marriage Selection," *Amer. J. Sociology*, **38**, 214-224 (1932).

[c] R. Abrams, "Residential Propinquity as a Factor in Marriage Selection": Fifty Year Trends in Philadelphia, *Amer. Soc. Review*, **8**, 288-294 (1943). Both cited in Boalt and Janson, *op. cit.*

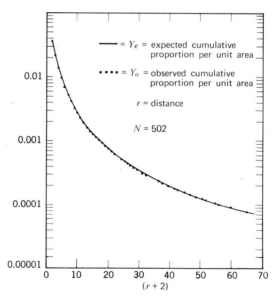

FIGURE 7

TABLE 5

Bullock (Unit 0.5 Mile)

	Assailant-Victim		Assailant-Offense		Victim-Offense	
		cum P		cum P		cum P
r	Percent	r^2	Percent	r^2	Percent	r^2
1	46.7	.149	57.0	.181	61.0	.194
2	10.8	.0458	10.0	.0533	14.3	.0599
3	5.8	.0224	5.0	.0255	8.2	.0295
4	6.9	.0140	2.2	.0148	3.9	.0174
5	4.1	.00946	2.8	.00980	2.8	.0115
6	1.1	.00667	1.5	.00694	1.1	.00807
7	3.0	.00509	2.8	.00528	2.6	.00610
8	2.8	.00404	1.7	.00413	1.5	.00474
9	1.1	.00323	1.3	.00331	1.3	.00380
10	1.1	.00265	0.4	.00270	0.6	.00310
11	0.2	.00220	0.2	.00223	0.6	.00256
12	1.5	.00188	0.6	.00189	0.2	.00217
13	0.9	.00162	0.6	.00140	0.4	.00186
14	0.4	.00140	0.2		0.4	.00161
?	13.6		13.7		1.1	
	100.00		100.00		100.00	

[a] H. A. Bullock, *op. cit.*, pp. 565-575.

[b] Distance between residence of assailant and residence of victim, residence of assailant and place of occurrence, and residence of victim and place of occurrence for 489 criminal homicides in Houston, Texas, 1945-1949.

SUMMARY

The delinquent offender resides close to the location of his offense. This is true in spite of the type of offense committed or the presence or absence of accomplices. However, there does appear to be a falling off within a block of his residence particularly for certain types of offenses (identifiable property thefts?).

If the delinquent lives close to his offense, there would be little difference between defining a high delinquency area in terms of offender's residence or offense location. A program designed to lower the number of delinquents in an area could reasonably expect a drop in the number of delinquencies in that area. And ecological studies of high delinquency areas can thus have some measure of confidence that the social characteristics of the high offense areas actually refer to the offenders who committed the offenses.

However, there is certainly more to crime and distance than this study indicates: certain types of offenses might not obey the above equation—for example, white-collar crime and professional crime. However, it might be that such offenses merely involve a larger threshold value (k in the above equation).

3

The Ecology of Delinquency

STANLEY TURNER

The purpose of the research described in the following pages was to locate the census tracts in Philadelphia which were high in juvenile delinquency in 1960 and, having located them, to find which variables contained in the U.S. Census of Philadelphia in 1960 were associated with the delinquency status of these tracts. Two kinds of high delinquency areas, that is, comprising bundles of high delinquency tracts, were identified: (1) those in which an unduly high proportion of juvenile offenders reside; and (2) those in which an unduly high proportion of delinquencies were committed.

A relatively new multivariate technique, Predictive Attribute Analysis (PAA), was used to determine which variables should be selected to "predict" areas high in delinquency.

CHOICE OF GEOGRAPHICAL UNIT

The first problem faced in trying to describe the spatial distribution of offenses was the choice of a geographical unit. What sort of unit should be chosen? Size of unit is important; if the unit chosen is too small (e.g., a square inch) no offense could be committed there; if, on the other hand, it is too large (e.g., all of Philadelphia), areas radically different in their delinquency rates would be combined. In the present case, we were interested in the delinquent neighborhood, and it was assumed that a neighborhood could be viewed as a bundle composed of several census tracts. This means that a group of contiguous census tracts with similar delinquency rates could be combined to form a "neighborhood."

There are certain objections to this procedure. Census tracts may be (1) too large, (2) vary in size, and (3) combine heterogeneous populations. However, according to the census,[1] "Tract boundaries were . . . generally designed to be relatively uniform with respect to

---

[1] U.S. Bureau of Census. U.S. Censuses of Population and Housing: 1960. **Census Tracts**. Final Report PHC(1)—116, U.S. Government Printing Office, Washington, D. C., 1962, p. 1.

population characteristics, economic status, and living conditions." Thus, for the purpose of roughly sketching in the pattern of delinquency in Philadelphia, census tracts were considered to be adequate. At any rate, all 377 census tracts listed in the 1960 census were examined. Of these, seven tracts had no area and referred to crews of vessels. These tracts were eliminated, as well as seventeen tracts with less than 100 total population and two tracts[2] that lacked relevant data. Most of the disregarded tracts had very few persons living in them; they tended to be parks or devoted to some other special use.

THE CHOICE OF OFFENDERS OR OFFENSES

The second problem was how to measure the delinquency of a tract. Two possible approaches suggested themselves. A high delinquency area could be either (a) one in which many delinquents live or (b) one in which many delinquent events occur. A measure based on the residence of delinquents might indicate the "delinquent productivity" of an area, while a measure based on the location of offenses might reveal the "dangerousness" of an area or its "consumption of delinquency." Instead of selecting one of these approaches, which after all have quite different uses and quite different meanings, both were used.

More exactly, the following method was employed to determine which tracts had an unduly large number of resident juvenile delinquents:

1. The number of juvenile offenders in each tract was computed (if an offender appeared in more than one offense, he was counted each time).

2. The number of persons under 18 years of age (the juvenile population) was computed.

3. The population was divided into the number of offenders; this resulted in the "offender rate."

4. The offender rate for each tract was compared to the offender rate for the city as a whole.

5. If the offender rate for the tract was higher than the citywide average, the tract was high in offenders; if not, it was low.

A similar procedure was followed to determine the offense rate for each tract, using the number of offenses that occurred in it. It should be noted, however, that when measuring offenders, no tract was counted as being high in offenders unless it had more than three resident offenders.

---

[2] These two hold the navy yard and the filter plant and lacked relevant income or housing data.

This was done to try to offset a bias in the data; the sample of offenders was a cluster sample because if an offense was selected, all offenders participating in it were also selected. Since such participants probably live near one another, they probably live in the same census tract. It is difficult to see how to offset this bias, and it may be that the scheme adopted does not aid in this regard. The technique used here seemed to present a map of offender concentration that looked better than the "uncorrected" form. Of course, no such technique was needed or used to compute the offense rates.

THE SAMPLE OF OFFENDERS AND OFFENSES

The data used in this study were taken from a ten percent systematic sample of all juvenile offenses known to the police in Philadelphia in 1960. From this group of 1313 offenses, all of those were selected that involved any physical injury, property loss, or property damage to a victim. This procedure yielded 504 offenses involving 950 offenders. A detailed explanation of the selection of the sample is found in Sellin and Wolfgang's *The Measurement of Delinquency*.[3]

Offenses involving injury, loss, or damage were recommended as a basis for measuring changes in delinquency by Sellin and Wolfgang. They called such offenses "index" offenses and argued forcefully that such offenses are less affected by changing legal definitions or police activity and have a higher presumed reportability than the whole class of offenses called juvenile delinquencies. In addition, such offenses have other characteristics that make them desirable for the present study.

1. *Almost all index offenses have a meaningful location.* Some offenses like conspiracy, truancy, runaway, incorrigibility, intoxication, etc., have no specific location or at any rate they have no clear, common-sense location. There was no, or little, difficulty in deciding the approximate location of the selected offenses.

2. *Index offenses tend to be more serious,* or at least, tend to be viewed as more serious than the offenses not selected. It is certainly more useful to know the spatial distribution of serious offenses then of trivial offenses or "juvenile status" offenses.

---

[3] Thorsten Sellin and Marvin E. Wolfgang, *The Measurement of Delinquency* (New York: John Wiley & Sons, Inc., 1964), 423 pp.

DETERMINING HIGH OFFENDER AREAS

In Map 1, each census tract high in offenders is shaded. It was assumed that some of these tracts were higher than average due to "chance" and did not represent a "real" delinquency neighborhood. In an attempt to remove this effect of chance variation, the following rule was adopted: All islands will be colored the same as the surrounding area. An island is a group of one, two, or three census tracts. Thus, to stand alone, an area must consist of four or more census tracts. If an island consists of three or fewer tracts of the opposite color, or by border, then it is swallowed up by the surrounding area. This rule was sufficient in all cases encountered in the present study, but it is possible to think of cases where the rule would be ambiguous. For example:

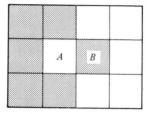

No side of tract *A* touches any other tract of the same color; therefore, tract *A* should be colored the same as the surrounding dark tracts. But the same applies to tract *B*. Therefore the rule does not specify which color tracts *A* and *B* should be. The rule that would have been followed in this case would have been: Compute the rate for *A* and *B* combined. If it is above average, shade both *A* and *B*; otherwise make both *A* and *B* white.

The application of the above rule (hereafter called the "smoothing" rule) to Map 1 simplified the distribution of delinquent offenders; this can be seen in Map 2. In this map, only four areas remain that are higher in resident juvenile offenders than citywide average.

The next step was to predict these areas on the basis of routine information.

CHOICE OF INFORMATION TO USE AS PREDICTORS

The census was the source of information used as predictors. From all such information that might have been used, the following were selected, pertaining to the population in census tracts: (1) percent of

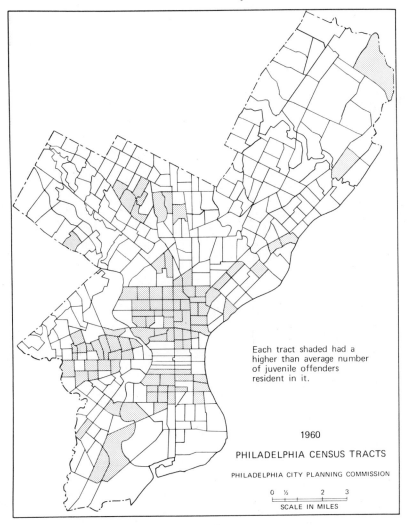

Each tract shaded had a higher than average number of juvenile offenders resident in it.

1960

PHILADELPHIA CENSUS TRACTS

PHILADELPHIA CITY PLANNING COMMISSION

0   ½   2   3
SCALE IN MILES

MAP 1

Census tracts of Philadelphia 1960, shaded to show high offender areas (based on police data).

Negroes; (2) family income; (3) family and unrelated income; (4) value of house; (5) migration; (6) unemployment; (7) density; (8) education; and (9) occupation.

These variables may need some explanation:

1. *Percent Negroes.* The census provides data on the number of Negroes, Whites, and other races in each tract. In 1960 there were 529,240

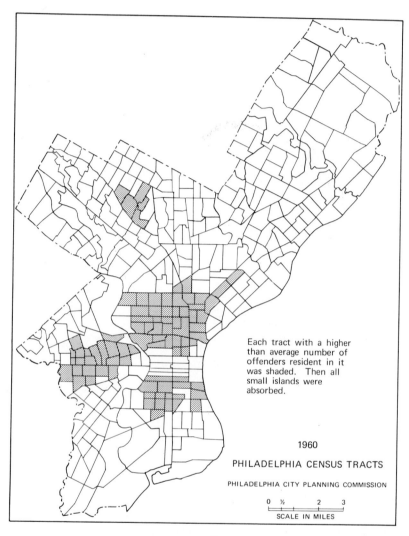

Each tract with a higher than average number of offenders resident in it was shaded. Then all small islands were absorbed.

1960

PHILADELPHIA CENSUS TRACTS

PHILADELPHIA CITY PLANNING COMMISSION

0   ½   2   3

SCALE IN MILES

MAP 2

High offender areas (based on police data).

Negroes in a total population of 2,002,512. Thus Negroes constituted 26.4 percent of Philadelphia's population.

2. *Family Income.* Information for the calendar year of 1959 was collected for all persons over 14 years of age. The income of a family consisting of two or more related persons living in the same household was called family income. Median family income was $5782.

3. *Family and Unrelated Income.* This added an unrelated individual's income to family income defined above. An unrelated individual resided in a household but was not kin to the family.

4. *Value of House.* This was based on the figure given by the respondent for one housing unit of an owner-occupied property. The respondent estimated how much the property would be worth in 1960. Median house value was $8700.

5. *Migration.* This was defined as the percentage of persons over five years of age living in a house different from that in which they lived in 1955. Forty-one percent met this requirement.

6. *Unemployment.* A male was unemployed if he was 14 years of age or over and was looking for work. There were 34,191 such males in a labor force of 532,208. Thus a little over 6 percent were unemployed.

7. *Density.* Density was defined as the total population divided by size of area. The census does not give the size of the area of census tracts so far as the present writer knows. This information could be derived from a map, but in the present case it was available from the Philadelphia City Planning Commission. The total area of Philadelphia was 129.714 square miles and the total population 2,002,512. Thus the mean number of persons per square mile was 15,438.

8. *Education.* Data on the years of school completed for all persons over 25 indicated that the median was 9.6 school years.

9. *Occupation.* This referred to the principal occupation of each employed male. The figure used in the present study was the proportion of "white-collar" workers of all employed persons. Professionals, managers, officials, proprietors, and technical, clerical, and sales workers were called white-collar workers. Craftsmen, foremen, operatives, private household workers, service workers, laborers, and those with unreported occupation were put into the residual category. There were 175,038 white-collar workers out of a total of 498,017 employed males, or an average of 35 percent.

Most variables were treated as dichotomies, but three were broken down into finer categories. Table 1 shows the detailed breakdowns and relevant class limits for all variables.

CHOICE OF TECHNIQUE FOR DATA ANALYSIS

Our task was to predict the delinquency of a tract from certain selected variables. How could this best be done? Certain criteria were needed.

TABLE 1

Variables Used to Predict Delinquency, Their Class Limits, and Frequencies

Dimension	Degree		Tracts Number
Nonwhite	Lowest	0 — 9.99%	225
(percent)	Lower	10.00— 26.79	31
	Higher	26.80— 49.99	27
	Highest	50.00—100.00	68
Family income	Lowest	0 —$3825.2	27
	Lower	3825.2 — 5781.7	117
	Higher	5781.7 — 8185.9	172
	Highest	8185.9 — +	35
Family and	Low	0 —$4789	124
unrelated income	High	4789 — +	227
Value of house	Low	0 —$8700.0	185
	High	8700.0 — +	166
Migration	Low	0 — 41%	145
	High	41% —100	206
Unemployment	Low	0 — 6.4%	213
(percent)	High	6.4%—100.0	138
Density per	Lowest	0 —15,437.9	134
square mile	Moderate	15,437.9 —35,000.0	117
	Highest	35,000.0 — +	100
Education	Low	0 — 9.6	191
(School Year)	High	9.6 — +	160
Occupation	Low	0 —35.1%	166
(white-collar)	High	35.1 — +	185

1. *Emphasis was to be on prediction.* The term prediction is not quite accurate since the "prediction" was made after the fact. It would be more accurate to say "specification," since that is what was really being done—tracts were specified as delinquent or not—and to use the word "prediction" for specification before the fact. At any rate, our interest was to specify *one* variable from a knowledge of the remaining variables; or, in other words, to specify the dependent variable from a host of independent ones. The important point to grasp is that *not all relations*

among all variables are important but just those between the independent variables and the dependent variable. Although the independent variables may relate in many interesting ways to each other, this is not important unless it affects the way they are related to the dependent variable.

2. *Many variables were used as the basis for prediction.* If only one variable had been used as a predictor, any measure of association would probably have been satisfactory. But since it was felt that the job to be done required many predictors, this narrowed the choice of technique. It is probably true that to predict delinquency, at least at present, many variables must be used.

3. *The dependent variable was viewed as a nominal scale.* Census tracts were viewed as falling into one of two categories: delinquent or not. Thus the aim was to *identify* delinquent areas and not to assess *how* delinquent they were. Certainly, to assess the degree of delinquency is important, but the task at hand was not that ambitious; it was merely to identify and specify delinquent neighborhoods and, therefore, the dependent variables were viewed as a dichotomy. Many variables considered in relation to individuals are certainly normally viewed as nominal scales—race, sex, delinquency—and the type of analysis selected was thought suitable to deal with such cases.

4. *Emphasis was on how well the job of prediction could be done.* The technique used should indicate the degree of success in predicting. Some measures imply that a set of results is or is not "due to chance." This is all very well but, in some cases, small differences may be called significant. The probability of a difference of results does not say anything about the size of the difference. This led us to select a measure of association. In other words, what was needed was a statistic measuring the degree of successful prediction.

5. *Measures chosen should have operational significance.* Some techniques provide numbers that describe associations but they are difficult if not impossible to describe in terms of operational significance. The measure chosen ought to describe how well a job of predicting is carried out by providing a number with an operational interpretation.[4]

The technique chosen was Predictive Attribute Analysis and the statistic used was Goodman and Kruskal's tau b and lambda b.[5] It was felt that this met the above criteria.

---

[4] Herbert Costner, "Criteria for Measures of Association," *American Sociological Review*, 30, 341-353 (June 1965).

[5] Leo A. Goodman and William H. Krushal, "Measures of Association for Cross Classification, II: Further Discussion and References," *Journal of the American Statistical Association*, 54, 123-163 (March 1959).

Since PAA is not well known, this technique could be described as follows:

1. Select any independent variable and measure its association with the dependent variable.
2. Repeat this for all other independent variables.
3. Select that variable that has the strongest association.
4. Split the sample into two parts: the cases that have the attribute and those that lack it. Call these parts branches.
5. Select either branch.
6. Repeat step C on all branches until a stopping point is reached.

In other words, the procedure splits the total group of cases into two groups on the basis of which variable bears the strongest association to the criterion. Each subgroup is then split on the same basis. The result of this process somewhat resembles a tree with branches. The trunk is the whole sample; the last twigs are the end groupings.

In the present case, the variable to be "predicted" was delinquency, and the information used to "predict" it was largely derived from the census. Thus the task was: How well can we "predict" whether a tract is above or below the average in delinquency by using information obtained from the census?

We chose a statistic and a stopping rule (to be discussed later), and PAA then considered each variable in turn and chose the one that best predicted delinquency. This split the sample into two parts. Each part was then considered separately and split or not according to the stopping rule. The results of this process can be seen on page 40.

PAA applies when interest lies in predicting a given attribute from a welter of other attributes when the attributes are intercorrelated and where the effects of a variable are increased or decreased by the presence or absence of other variables.[6]

LIMITATIONS OF PAA[7]

1. PAA is not certain to detect all interactions. The only sure way to find all of them is to form 2^{k-1} subsets and use a sufficient number of cases. But with k at all large this is impossible.

---

[6] More exactly PAA applies when you have n events simultaneously classified on k nominal scales and where k is large compared to n. And, furthermore, the aim is to specify the value of one attribute from the knowledge of the other k-1 attributes where interactions and intercorrelations are suspected.

[7] Leslie T. Wilkins and P. McNaughton-Smith, "New Prediction and Classification Methods in Criminology," *The Journal of Research in Crime & Delinquency*, 1, 19-32 (January 1964).

2. PAA may also miss really important predictive factors which occur too late in the splitting sequence when the n is too small.

3. It will also fail to detect offsetting interactions between two variables where neither variable has an effect alone. That is, it assumes that if the simultaneous presence of two variables is associated with the criterion then at least one of them must be associated by itself.

4. PAA maximizes specification or prediction only. It does not detect the most general differences if they are unrelated to prediction. That is, it is not concerned with all the interrelations between all variables but only in the relations of all other variables to the criterion.

5. PAA is limited by the manner the information is coded. In the case of "natural" dichotomies there is little or no problem, but if a continuous variable is coded into only two classes, then whether this variable will be useful in predicting will depend in part on where the cutting point is set. Thus, predictive power may be lost if the original data are coded into too few classes.

6. PAA suffers from an "overfitting" bias; it capitalizes on chance variation. McNaughton-Smith points out that this can be handled by a split-half technique.[8]

ADVANTAGES OF PAA

1. PAA is best used when there are many variables in which nonlinear effects are present or suspected and in which unanticipated interactions may exist. Furthermore, it deals with the problem of interrelatedness of items. PAA analysis prevents one from using as predictors variables that are related to the criterion but do not add anything to predictive power when used in conjunction with other variables. That is, PAA does not allow "dead wood" to be used.

2. PAA is relatively easy to do. Data processing can be done using a desk calculator and either a sorter with a pocket counter or an IBM accounting machine. Of course, if n or k become too large a computer has a real advantage.

The two main parts of PAA are the splitting rule that tells which subdivisions are to be made and the stopping rule that tells when the subdivision is to stop. Each of these will be discussed in turn.

---

[8] P. McNaughton-Smith, *Some Statistical and Other Numerical Techniques for Classifying Individuals,* London, Her Majesty's Stationery Office, 1965.

The Splitting Rule

The splitting rule is based on some selected statistic. Which one should be chosen? There is probably no "best" choice but rather an optimum choice for a given purpose. The interest and aim of the present task was to "predict" whether or not a tract was high in delinquency. Thus, some measure that considers how well prediction can be improved was needed. This led to the selection of Goodman and Kruskal tau b,[9] which measures *the relative decrease in the number of mistakes*[10] *in predicting B when A is known, compared to the number of mistakes made in predicting B when A is not known subject to certain restrictions.* Since all variables were coded as dichotomies, all the associations were in the form of 2 x 2 tables.

The Stopping Rule

If this procedure were allowed to continue without end the tree would become unwieldy; there might be subgroups with only one case in each. To prevent this, some restriction is placed on the splitting procedure. This restriction is called the stopping rule. Many possible stopping rules could be proposed. The one we chose was to stop when the proposed split failed to reduce the number of mistakes by a set percentage of the original number of mistakes. If at the start there were a certain number of mistakes made in predicting the dependent variable, then no split would follow that did not reduce this number of mistakes by a chosen percent. In the present case there were about 132 mistakes made in predicting whether or not 351 tracts were high or low in delinquency. We arbitrarily chose 1.5 percent as the stopping point. Thus, no split was made that did not reduce the mistakes made by 1.98 (1.5 percent of 131.87). Note that the stopping rule is based on importance rather than significance. A significant split might be rejected if it were unimportant.

An additional rule was imposed on the size of the final groups. It was felt that a split might be important (as measured above) yet suggest a final group that was too small. A very liberal rule was adopted in this case; we set five as the minimal size of a final group. It would be preferable if the final group size were larger (say around 25), but this was not practical in the present study.

---

[9] And if tau b is computed for a 2 x 2 table it is equivalent to phi square, the mean square contingency, which is easier to compute.

[10] A "mistake" is predicting a tract to be delinquent when it is not or predicting a tract a nondelinquent when it is.

RUN 1—PREDICTING HIGH OFFENDER AREAS

The results of the first analysis are shown in Run 1. At the first level, the entire sample of 351 cases is represented. All possible 2 x 2's were examined; the 2 x 2 with the highest degree of association was selected. In fact, the best split was for those below the mean of the city and those above the mean of the city in the proportion of Negroes. This is shown in Table 2.

TABLE 2

The First Split: Tracts Classified by Racial Composition and Delinquency

All Census Tracts	Lower than Average in Delinquency	Higher than Average in Delinquency	Total
High in Negroes	21	67	88
Low in Negroes	235	28	263
Total	256	95	351

The first split was made on race because this variable had the maximum association with the dependent variable, that is, knowledge of the racial composition of a tract enabled us to predict the crime rate better than any other single variable. (It should not be thought that this means that the variable of racial composition is indispensable; it could be that some other complex of variables could do the job of predicting as well.) Thus, this variable is the basis of the first split in Fig. 1. The numbers in the blocks indicate the number of census tracts and the percentage of these tracts that are above the city average in delinquency. At the start there were 351 tracts, of which 25 percent were above the average in delinquency. The numbers outside the boxes represent the number of mistakes reduced by using the following variable. Thus, splitting on the basis of racial composition enabled us to reduce the number of mistakes made in predicting delinquency by 53.8 mistakes. Note, furthermore, that the tree does not split everywhere on the same variables—for instance, tracts low in Negroes split on income, but tracts high in Negroes split on density. This means that there is interaction between the variables (the effects of income are not uniform across the tree but only in certain branches).

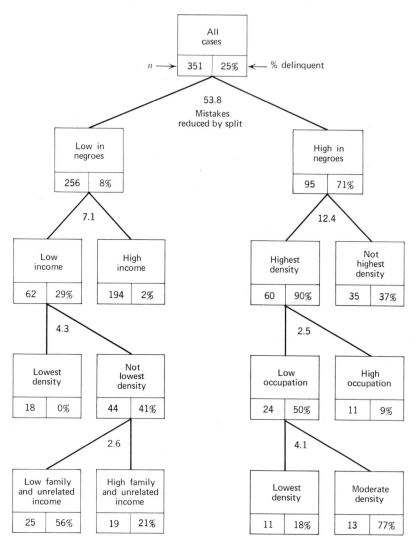

FIGURE 1

Run 1: Predictive attribute analysis of areas high in resident offenders.

Interpretation

The following variables were important, that is, they appear in the tree and were used as the basis for splitting groups: (a) racial proportion; (b) family income; family and unrelated income; (c) density; (d) occupation. The following variables could have been the basis for splits but did not appear: (a) house value; (b) migration; (c) unemployment; (d) education. Density appears to have an effect on both high white and high Negro areas and the direction of its effect is consistent (higher density is always associated with higher delinquency). The direction of association is similar to what would be expected for the remaining variables: low occupation, low income, and low family and unrelated income all are associated with high delinquency.

Two questions are raised by the pattern in the tree from Run 1:

1. *Why does the variable of racial proportion seem important?* This will be analyzed in Run 2.

2. *Why does density seem important?* There are many possible explanations, but one may be considered. If delinquents go only a fixed distance to commit offenses and this distance is independent of population, there will be more victims available in high density areas, and this effect may not be removed by dividing the area in square miles by population.

The splitting process stopped as indicated in the diagram and thus each terminal branch represents a final grouping. The final groupings are rearranged for easy reading in Table 3. This table lists each of the eight terminal branches from the tree just discussed but in a different form. The eight groups are listed by their proportion delinquent. The most delinquent group was high in Negroes and high in density; 54 of the 60 tracts in this group were above the average in delinquency. The second most delinquent group was high in Negroes, moderate in density, and low in occupation; the third most delinquent group was low in Negroes, moderate to high in density, low in family income, and low in family and unrelated income. The rest of the groups were below the average in delinquency. This suggests that we could lump together all those above the average in delinquency (the first three groups) and lump all those below the average (the last five groups).

The next step was to create a map, using the predictions. Each tract high in delinquency was shaded and each low tract left blank. The same rule about smoothing the data (eliminating small islands) that was used on the map of observed delinquent cases was used to make the map of predicted delinquent areas. The final form of the map is shown (Map 3) and may be compared to the observed delinquency areas (Map 2).

The predicted map is similar to the observed map. But in comparing them, we see that the small group to the north on the observed map is missing from the predicted map. There is some indication that this is a relatively new delinquency area and, being new, it is small. This makes

TABLE 3

Final Sets from Run 1 Listed in Order of Percent High in Offenders [a]

Percent Negroes	Density	Typology Family income	Family and unrelated income	Occupation	Number of Tracts Above and Below Average +	−	Total	Percent Tracts Above Average
High Negroes	Highest density				54	6	60	90
High Negroes	Moderate density			Low occupation	10	3	13	77
High Whites	Moderate to high density	Low income	Low family and unrelated income		14	11	25	56
High Whites	Moderate or high density	Low income	High family and unrelated income		4	15	19	21
High Negroes	Lowest density			Low occupation	2	9	11	18
High Negroes	Moderate or low density			High occupation	1	10	11	9
High Whites		High income			3	191	194	2
High Whites	Lowest density	Low income			0	18	18	0
					88	263	351	25

a All sets are taken from Fig. 1.

it hard to detect using the smoothing procedure adopted here. The remaining areas seem to be indicated well enough. In fact one could determine exactly how well the two maps agree. Each tract can be simultaneously classified as predicted high or low in delinquent offenders and as observed high or low in offenders. This gives rise to the following table (Table 4).

Goodman and Kruskal's lambda b was chosen to measure how well the predictive scheme worked. It measures the relative decrease in mistakes when the knowledge of a variable is added. Thus it measures the proportional reduction of errors in predicting B when A is known compared to A not known. In the case of Table 4, 88 mistakes would be made if only the marginal distributions of the column totals were known but, knowing the typology, one would only make $14 + 12 = 26$ mistakes. Thus lambda b is

$$\lambda b = \frac{88 - 26}{88} = 0.70$$

The specific measures of association reported here should be interpreted with even more care than is usually the case. They are probably overstated for at least two reasons.

TABLE 4

The Association between Maps 2 and 3*

From Map 2

	All Census Tracts	Lower than Average in Delinquency	Higher than Average in Delinquency	Total
Predicted higher than average in delinquency	76	14		90
Predicted lower than average in delinquency	12	268		280
Total	88	282		370

$\lambda_b = 0.70$

* Map 2 shows areas observed to be high in delinquent offenders and Map 3 those areas predicted to be high in delinquent offenders.

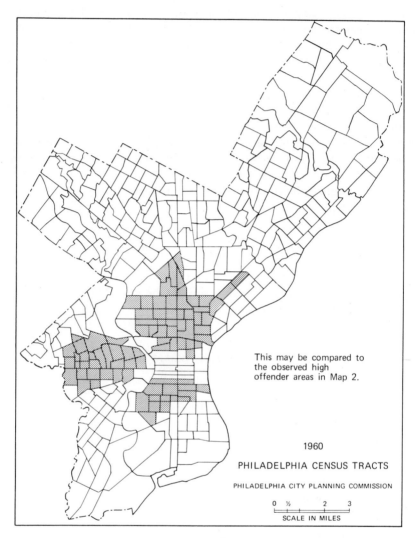

This may be compared to the observed high offender areas in Map 2.

1960

PHILADELPHIA CENSUS TRACTS

PHILADELPHIA CITY PLANNING COMMISSION

0   ½   2   3

SCALE IN MILES

MAP 3
Predicted high offender areas: Run 1 (based on census data).

First, PAA suffers from an overfitting bias; it capitalizes on chance variation. As McNaughton-Smith points out, this can usually be corrected by dividing the sample into two parts at random, generating the predictive attribute analysis on one half, determining the final sets, and then applying those sets to the second half to find out how well typology predicts. Such a technique would provide, it seems, unbiased estimates. But this technique could not be used in the present case.

Second, a bias is introduced by the smoothing procedure. This procedure, while simplifying graphic presentation, does involve a cost, since each tract is not independently tested. We propose to examine this bias by eliminating the smoothing procedure and testing how well the predictive scheme works without it.

Summary of Run 1

Certain clusters of tracts in Philadelphia were identified as being higher than average in the proportion of resident juvenile offenders. There were four such clusters in the city. These areas could be specified fairly well by a knowledge of five variables obtained from routine census information. One principal question was raised (but not answered): Why does the variable of race appear important? Certainly *any* variable that conveys information is useful in some sense; but the variable of race is unsatisfactory because it is a *fixed* attribute, and fixed attributes (like birth date, sex, etc.) are useful only in identifying persons; they are dead-end attributes from the point of view of programs designed to reduce delinquency. What is needed is a set of variables (like income, density, education) that can be manipulated. Since the other eight variables were all "manipulable," it was decided to rerun the whole analysis but hold out the variable of race. This was the strategy behind Run 2.

RUN 2—EXCLUDING RACE AS A VARIABLE

Could the remaining variables specify delinquency as well or almost as well, or does racial proportion enable us to predict better with than without it? Can we replace the variable race with another set of variables and thus gain a clue to what race stands for in relation to delinquency? That was done in Run 2 simply by ignoring information on racial proportion and using the rest of the variables in the analysis. The results produced the tree shown in Fig. 2.

When race is ignored, density is the first variable to split the sample. Income also appears in the tree just as it did in Run 1; but a new variable—house value—appears.

Run 2 produced five terminal sets, with two of them higher than the citywide average in resident offenders. Thus of the 67 tracts with the highest density and low house value, 88 percent were higher than average in resident offenders. Of the 33 tracts with moderate density and low income, 48 percent were higher. On the other hand, those areas that

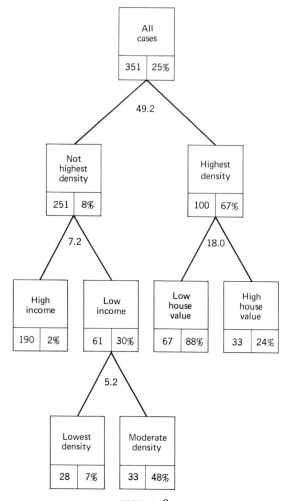

FIGURE 2

Run 2: Predictive attribute analysis of areas high in resident offenders—the variable of race held out.

lacked highest density and had high income were rarely high in resident offenders. In fact, only 2 percent of such tracts were high.

We can construct a map by combining both high areas (67 + 33 = 100 tracts) and, employing the same smoothing technique as previously, determine to what extent the map from Run 2 correlates with the observed high resident offender map (Map 2). To save space, the map is not included, but it does suggest the areas fairly well. The measure of association, lambda — *b* in this case, is 0.57.

This means that by omitting racial composition from the equations we can reduce the number of mistakes in predicting high resident offender areas by 57 percent. It will be recalled that by including racial composition we could reduce mistakes by 70 percent. Many of the mistakes that were reduced by the knowledge of racial composition could be accounted for by the ensemble of other variables. Racial composition, then, does convey information about offender areas but by no means as much as might have appeared from a superficial analysis of Run 1.

Run 2 produced five terminal groups (see Fig. 9). Since racial composition does convey some information, it could be asked which, if any, of those five terminal groups are related to racial composition. That is to say, if we reintroduced racial composition, would it split any of the five terminal groups? This would be a stringent test of the importance of racial composition, at least for the present data.

RUN 3 — REINTRODUCTION OF RACIAL COMPOSITION

Each of the five terminal groups of Run 2 was tested against racial composition. Where the association was strong enough, further splits were made and the splitting process was allowed to go as far as it could, subject only to the stopping rule. Only two further splits were made, and each of these turned out to be final groups. Thus, instead of five terminal groups Run 3 produced seven terminal groups. The two previously established groups which split on racial composition were: (1) areas with low income and moderate density and (2) areas with highest density and high house value.

A smoothed map was created from the data of Run 2 by combining all tracts high in resident offenders (6 + 67 + 25 + 8 = 106) and proceeding as before. The lambda-b in this case was 0.60.

From the three runs we can conclude that:

1. Allowing all the variables to enter into the prediction equations, we can specify high offender areas fairly well. In fact, we can reduce our mistakes in predicting high resident offender areas by 70 percent.

2. If we omit race as a variable, we can predict less well but the other variables can still account for some of the mistakes that racial composition previously accounted for. In this case, we reduce mistakes by 57 percent.

3. If we reintroduce racial composition, after having previously excluded it, we explain a few more mistakes but not as many as we did by

using the original (optimal) typology. In this case, the mistakes are reduced by 60 percent.

4. Points 1, 2, and 3 above imply that racial composition accounts for a small amount of the total number of mistakes in a way not accounted for by the ensemble of other variables. Or, in other words, the variable of racial composition cannot be completely replaced, without predictive loss, by any set of our remaining variables as coded.

If we could determine what the variable of racial composition stood for, we could replace it by a set of explanatory variables and predict delinquency on that basis. This would be valuable because: (a) the weight of criminological thinking is against using race as an explanatory variable; (b) race is a fixed attribute that cannot be manipulated by any action program; and (c) since there are countries that have racial homogeneity and yet have crime, race evidently is not a necessary variable in the occurrence of delinquency. For these three reasons, it seems important to suggest how the search could be extended for a set of variables that can completely replace racial composition. Sonnquist and Morgan[11] suggest some techniques. These are:

1. *Recode the variables used.* The variables used were coded into two, three, or four segments on each dimension. It could be that if the cutting points were placed differently or if the raw data were more finely coded, the resulting groups would predict better.

2. *Add fresh information.* No predictive technique will work unless the relevant information is fed into it. Perhaps we have ignored or overlooked certain variables.

3. *Look-ahead technique.* Perhaps the variable sought for is a combination of two or more variables that have been included. Perhaps a pair of variables could split the tree when no single variable could. What this amounts to is to look one step beyond what the stopping rule would ordinarily allow.

Certain considerations are involved in using each of these techniques. Some discussion of them may be justified. The first suggestion is interesting but how does one recode and in what fineness of detail? It would seem that the variable might be suggested by an examination of the entire tree with an eye toward locating any variable that *almost* split different parts of the tree but never appeared in the tree. Such a

---

[11] John A. Sonnquist and James N. Morgan, "Problems in the Analyses of Survey Data and a Proposal," *Journal of the American Statistical Association,* **58**, 415-434, (June 1963) and their *Detection of Interaction Effects,* Ann Arbor, Michigan, Survey Research Center, 1964, 292 pp.

"submerged" variable might be recoded. Or if a variable has almost split parts of the tree and did appear in the tree, it could be examined.

The second suggestion is promising but difficult. How does one know beforehand which variables are likely to be important? What prior criterion of relevance should one have? Unfortunately, all that appears as an answer is that the variables should come from theoretical deduction, other studies, or hunches. Perhaps the most practical suggestion is to add variables that other studies have found important.

The third suggestion is difficult to adopt if data handling is a problem. The present analysis was all conducted on an IBM accounting machine; this sharply limits the use of such techniques. Obviously this would present no problem to a computer.

Sonnquist and Morgan further point out what parts of the tree could most fruitfully be attacked by any of the techniques suggested. They observe that terminal groups do not give rise to further splits because (a) they are too small; (b) too homogeneous (contain too few mistakes); or (c) large and heterogeneous enough but no suggested split produces a strong enough correlation. It is clear that type (c) groups are the ones open to attack. Taking all the previous comments into account, it appears that fresh information concerning variables that other studies have found to be important should be run on the two groups split by racial proportion in Fig. 3. Such an effort is currently being undertaken.

TYPES OF OFFENSES TYPICAL OF HIGH OFFENDER AREAS

Thus far, we have considered highly delinquent areas as areas that were high in resident offenders. A further question may be raised as to what sorts of offenses are typical of high resident offender areas. All of the events considered thus far were "index events" in the sense described by Sellin and Wolfgang, that is, the events involving either physical injury or property loss or damage, and the only offenders thus far considered were those involved in such "index events." But it was felt that for more refined analysis a more detailed breakdown was needed. Therefore, the 504 index offenses were broken down into categories somewhat similar to the Uniform Crime Reporting scheme and then plotted into two groups: those occurring in one of the high resident offender areas and those occurring elsewhere. Table 5 displays in its first two columns the results of this procedure. Notice that all assaults are combined and that larcenies (since they are so numerous) are kept apart. In addition, 17

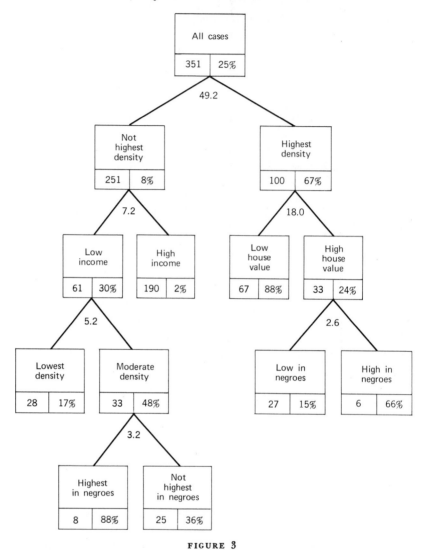

FIGURE 3

Run 3: Predictive attribute analysis of high resident offender areas—racial composition reintroduced.

index offenses spread throughout the Uniform Crime Reporting system are combined into one classification called "other" since they were so infrequent. The proportion of the total offenses occurring in each cell was then computed and presented in the column labeled "Proportion." Finally, to examine the effects of crime type independently of the fact

TABLE 5

All 504 Index Offenses Classified According to Their Uniform Crime Reporting System Type and Whether They Occurred in High Resident Offender Areas

Offenses	Number			Proportion		Adjusted Proportion	
	+ a	− b	Total	+	−	+	−
Homicide	2	0	2	.004	.001	.004	.000
Rape	3	2	5	.006	.004	.005	.004
Robbery	23	4	27	.046	.008	.041	.009
Assault	67	47	114	.133	.093	.119	.105
Burglary	50	23	73	.099	.046	.089	.052
Shoplifting	17	32	49	.034	.063	.030	.072
Auto accessories	9	16	25	.018	.032	.016	.036
Bicycle	11	10	21	.022	.020	.020	.022
Other larcenies	43	39	82	.085	.077	.076	.077
Auto theft	15	23	38	.030	.046	.027	.052
Malicious mischief	31	20	51	.062	.040	.055	.045
Other	10	7	17	.020	.014	.018	.016
Total	281	223	504	.599	.443	.500	.500

Offenses	+	−	Total
Larcenies	.169	.269	.438
Nonlarcenies	.331	.231	.562
Total	.500	.500	1.000

a Plus means that offense occurred in a high resident offender area.
b Minus means the offense did not occur in such an area.

that more offenses occur in the high crime areas, the proportion of offenses occurring in high and low offender areas was made equal, that is, the two marginal proportions (0.559 and 0.443) were adjusted to be 0.5000 each. The results of this process appear in the column labeled Adjusted Proportion; it shows that low offender areas are high in each form of larceny and high in no other offense compared to the high offender area. This suggests that a collapse of the table into larcenies and other offenses is justified. Such a collapsing permits the following summary:

Larcenies are "typical" of areas that are low in offenders; all other sorts of offenses are "typical" of areas that are high in offenders.

In particular, shoplifting, larceny of auto accessories, and auto theft are strongly characteristic of offensive events that occur in low offender areas. These events are all target offenses in that they require a car or store for them to occur. We already know that offenders do not travel very far to commit their offenses but that when they do travel a considerable distance, some target of the nature described above is usually involved.

SERIOUSNESS OF OFFENSIVE EVENTS IN HIGH OFFENDER AREAS

Another question considered was whether offensive events committed in high offender areas were more serious than offenses committed elsewhere?

To answer this question, each of the 504 events was classified by its seriousness score and by its place of occurrence. Following a suggestion made by Sellin and Wolfgang, only those offenses with a seriousness score of 2 or more were considered. This eliminates the most trivial offenses from the analysis. Table 6 shows the results of this precedure. Clearly, the more serious offenses tend to occur in high offender areas. This can be even more clearly shown by Fig. 4, which shows that the proportion of seriousness scores occurring in high offender areas increases with increasing seriousness.

OUT-MIGRATION FROM HIGH RESIDENT OFFENDER AREAS

A final question about high resident offender areas was considered: Do offenders who live in high offender areas commit offenses in that area or do they go to another area to commit offensive events? This question was answered by classifying each offender by the area in which he resided and by the area in which he committed his offensive event. The four high resident offender areas were labeled A, B, C, and D, and 930 of the 950 offenders provided complete enough information to be appropriately classified. Table 7 shows that offenders living in the four high resident offender areas left their own area to commit an offensive event in another high resident offender area in only 19 cases. When offenders left their own areas they did so by going to an area that was low in resident offenders. There is a very strong diagonal concentration in Table 7 showing that the offenses committed in such areas

TABLE 6

All Serious Offensive Events Classified by Degree of Seriousness and Place of Occurrence [a]

Seriousness Score of Event	Occurred in High Offender Areas	Occurred in Low Offender Areas	Total
2	89	94	183
3	35	12	47
4	38	18	56
5	8	5	13
6	5	0	5
7	7	8	15
8	1	0	1
9	1	0	1
10	0	0	0
11	1	1	2
12	0	0	0
13	0	0	0
14	3	1	4
15	0	0	0
16	1	0	1
.			
.			
.			
26	2	0	2
Total	191	139	330

[a] Two offenses had unknown locations and 172 offenses and seriousness scores of 1.

are committed by residents and not by migrants; but no statistical measure of association between area of residence and area of offense location was computed since the sample of offenders was a cluster sample and not a random sample (if any offender in an event was selected, all others were selected). Nonetheless, the degree of diagonal concentration seems strong.

RUN 4—PREDICTION OF HIGH OFFENSE AREAS

The previous section dealt with predicting the tracts that were high in *offenders;* the present section deals with predicting tracts that were high in *offenses*. These two notions complement each other. When an

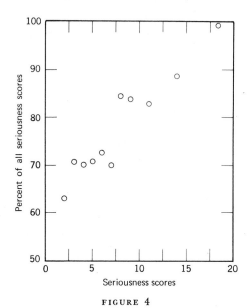

FIGURE 4

Percent of seriousness scores in high offenders areas at and above each degree of serious-ness (starting at seriousness score 2).

area is referred to as a high crime area, it could be one that "produces" criminals or one that "consumes" crimes. Since we know that offenders do not go very far to commit their offenses, the pattern derived from a study of offenses might be fairly similar to the pattern for offenders. At any rate, the same technique[12] used to generate the offender areas was used to generate the offense areas. Map 4 shows tracts higher than average in offenses. This map will be the target map used to predict high crime areas from the knowledge we have of census variables.

Map 4 is quite similar to the map based on offenders (Map 2). Yet there are some differences. The downtown or central area of the city is high in offenses but is not high in offenders. And the area to the southwest is similarly high in offenses but not high in offenders. The downtown area is high in larcenies (especially shoplifting). This section has many stores that have the effect of simultaneously attracting offenders and

---

[12] No lower limit on the number of offenses was imposed; it will be recalled that in an attempt to offset the bias of a cluster sample, the offender map was based on tracts which had to have at least four offenders in them. Since the offense sample was not clustered, no "correction" was needed. Furthermore, the number of offenses was divided by the *total* population, not the juvenile population. This statistic measures the number of juvenile index offenses per head of population and seems a more reasonable measure of the "consumption" of index events.

TABLE 7

The Area of Residence of Offenders and the Area in which Their Offense Occurred

			Offender's Residence				Total
			High in Offenders				Not High in Offenders
			A	B	C	D	
O f f e n s e l o c a t i o n	H i g h . i n o f f e n d e r s	A	17				6	23
		B	2	268	4		24	298
		C	1	1	80	7	19	108
		D		2	2	75	11	90
		Not high	10	73	45	39	244	411
		Total	30	344	131	121	304	930

reducing the resident population, thus accounting in a large part for the high offense rate and low offender rate.

The same set of census variables used to predict high resident offender areas was used to predict high offense areas. Fig. 5 shows the results. Family and unrelated income was the best single predictor of high offense areas and, therefore, the total sample was divided into two branches by using that variable. For areas with high income, house value was important but, for areas with low income, racial composition was important. The four sets resulting from the above divisions proved to be final sets—no other variable reduced the mistakes sufficiently to allow a split to be made. The highest offense areas were those characterized by

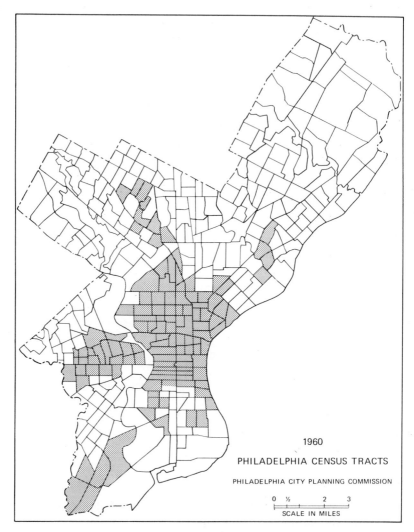

1960

PHILADELPHIA CENSUS TRACTS

PHILADELPHIA CITY PLANNING COMMISSION

0   ½   2   3
SCALE IN MILES

MAP 4
High offense areas (based on police data).

low family and unrelated income *and* high proportion of Negroes, while
the areas lowest in offenses were characterized by high family and unrelated income *and* high house value. About 86 percent of the tracts in
the highest group were higher than the citywide average in offenses
while only 4 percent of the tracts in the lowest group were higher.

A smoothed map, based on the above predictor variables, was then
constructed (Map 5) and compared to the map prepared from the ob-

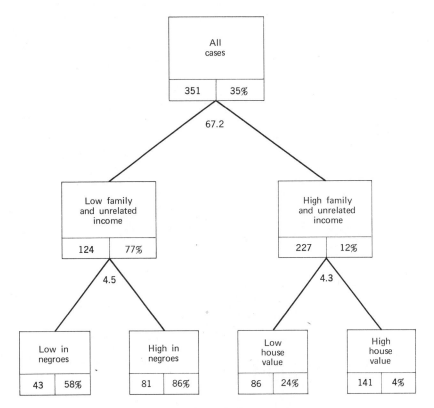

FIGURE 5
Run 4: Predictive attribute analysis of high offense areas.

served offense rates, and the degree of association between them was calculated. A knowledge of the predictor variables enabled us to reduce the number of mistakes in predicting high offense area by 53 percent $(\lambda_b = 0.53)$.

Intercorrelation of Offense and Offender Areas

The map of offense areas is somewhat similar to the map of offender areas. To what extent does the knowledge of one of these add to our ability to predict the other? Let us assume that the task is to predict offense areas. Using the offense typology to predict offense areas decreases the mistakes by about half $(\lambda = .50)$. If we add the offender typology to the offense typology, the number of mistakes is reduced by only one percent more. To sum up:

1. The offender typology predicts the offense areas to a limited extent.

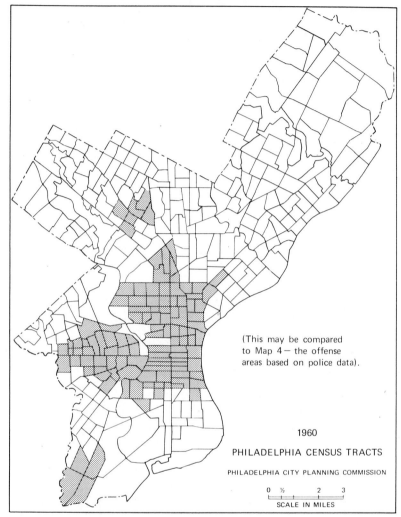

(This may be compared
to Map 4 — the offense
areas based on police data).

1960

PHILADELPHIA CENSUS TRACTS

PHILADELPHIA CITY PLANNING COMMISSION

0   ½   2   3

SCALE IN MILES

MAP 5

Tracts predicted to be high in offense (based on census information).

2. The offender typology when added to the offense typology yields almost nothing if the task is to predict offense areas.

3. *Lacking* offense information, offender information might yield a very rough picture of offense areas.

The above analysis suggests that offense areas may be thought of as made up of areas *high in offenses and offenders* or areas *high in offenses only*. The latter type represents an interesting group of offenses in its own right and some tentative explanations of such areas may be considered.

Explanations of High Offense Only Areas. Certain areas were high in offenses yet low in offenders. What makes an area have these characteristics? Of many possible hypotheses, the following were considered:

1. *Proximity.* When offenders travel to commit an offense they do not travel far.[13] This means that most of their offenses are committed close to their homes. Therefore, offense areas tend also to be offender areas. But those who do travel outside an offender area are again most likely to travel only a short distance. This would imply that areas high in offenses but low in offenders (Offense Only Areas) should be found around the borders of high offender areas. A special case of this would be an area that is between several high offender areas. This sort of area would strongly tend to be an Offense Only Area since it could draw from several offender areas.

2. *Push-Pull.* When offenders travel outside their offender areas they may do so because what the offender seeks may be concentrated in a place far from his residence. Examples of this would be areas with many stores or movies, and recreation areas which also may attract juveniles, yet have low resident populations. In addition, most people of juvenile age are in schools; if an area has a school and low resident population, it may appear to have a "high offense only" rate. Finally, an area may have many targets in it (bicycles, autos) and thus attract juveniles. If such areas have a low resident population, they too will appear to have a "high offense only" rate.

3. *Accessibility.* Transportation makes certain areas of the city easier to reach than others. Since juveniles travel by public transportation and proportionately own fewer cars, they probably travel to spots that are easy to reach. The Offense Only Area should be found in places that have many terminals of public transportation.

These three explanations fit the downtown section of Philadelphia, which has a relatively low juvenile population, lies between three high offender areas, has many stores, etc., and is the most accessible part of the city. In fact, all three explanations could be interpreted to fit a general explanation.

General Explanation

An area will be high in offenses but low in offenders when its effective population is much larger than its census (resident) population. Thus areas lying close to high offender areas will contain offenders that travel into it yet are not counted by the census, since they do not reside there. Areas with shops, stores, and theatres, etc., will have a higher effective population of juveniles than the census would indicate. Similarly, ac-

---

[13] See the preceding article.

cessible areas will have more juveniles present in it than the census indicates as residents. This general explanation is suggested but was not tested in any way.

SUMMARY

Census tracts that were high in juvenile delinquency in Philadelphia in 1960 were identified. The data on delinquency were taken from a ten percent systematic sample of all juvenile offenses known to the Philadelphia police in 1960, involved one or more offenders under 18 years of age, and produced physical injury, property loss, or property damage to a victim. This procedure yielded 504 offenses involving 950 offenders. Two kinds of areas were identified: those with an unduly high number of resident juvenile offenders and those in which an unduly high number of offenses were committed. A smoothing technique was developed to simplify the maps obtained from plotting such areas. Nine variables (racial proportion, family income, family and unrelated income, house value, migration, unemployment, density, education, and occupation) were used as predictor variables to specify high offense and offender areas. Predictive Attribute Analysis (a predictive technique that aims at uncovering nonlinear relations and interactions between a host of variables and a single criterion variable) was used as a technique. Racial composition, income, density, family and unrelated income, and occupation were the variables useful in predicting high resident offender areas. Eliminating racial composition from the analysis somewhat lowered the predictive efficiency, but suggestions were made for studying further the relation between racial composition and delinquency.

High resident offender areas were found to be high in most types of offensive events, especially crimes against the person, but were somewhat lower in larcenies. High resident offender areas were not only high in the number of offenses that occurred but were also the locale of more serious offenses. Only rarely did offenders leave their own area to commit offenses in another high offender area.

In predicting high offense areas, family and unrelated income, racial composition, and house value were the only important variables.

Since high offense areas also tend to be high resident offender areas, a new type of area was defined: areas high in offenses but low in resident offenders. It was suggested that such an area is characterized by the presence of many persons who are not residents, that is, a large effective population compared to its resident population.

4

The Delinquency of Gangs
and Spontaneous Groups

BERNARD COHEN

The field of criminology during the last fifteen years has been enhanced with numerous sociological theories that attempt to explain juvenile delinquency. It is significant and, at the same time, more than coincidental that the major concern of most of these theories, particularly those frequently cited in criminological literature, centers around gang delinquency.

The extensive and recent concern with gang delinquency reflects more than our discipline's expected interest in groups. Not only have consistent research findings reported that the vast bulk of juvenile delinquency occurs in groups,[1] but there is also unusual public concern with gangs reflected by the mass media of communication. Almost daily, large urban newspapers and radio and television networks report gang activity and incidents. Moreover, gangs have frequently been employed by the cinema and theater as their central theme. The most notable play of this type was the recent Broadway production of *West Side Story*, which still draws large audiences throughout the country.

In contrast to the many theories that attempt to explain gang behavior is the relative paucity of systematic data or ordered body of facts that might be used as a basis for testing the validity of their underlying concepts, propositions, and hypotheses. In particular, we need facts and patterns concerning the content, extent, and amount of harm caused by delinquent gangs and groups. Moreover, we require knowledge of the distribution of their patterns, that is, age, race, sex, prior criminal history and social class in the social structure. This information is essential

---

[1] For instance, C. R. Shaw and H. D. McKay found that only 18.2 percent out of a total of 5480 offenders committed their offenses alone. C. R. Shaw and H. D. McKay, "Social Factors in Juvenile Delinquency," National Commission on Law Observance and Enforcement, Report on the Cause of Crime, Vol. II (1931), pp. 195-196. Cited by D. R. Taft and R. W. England, Jr., *Criminology*, New York: The Macmillan Company, 1964 (4th ed.), p. 171. For other examples see S. Glueck and E. Glueck, *Delinquents in the Making*, New York: Harper, 1952, p. 89; W. C. Kvaraceus, "Social Aspects of Delinquent Behavior," *Journal of Social Hygiene*, November 1943, pp. 526-527.

not only for individual delinquents but collectively as well. Delinquent gangs and groups are sociocultural entities that cannot be explained by a description of patterns pertaining to their individual constituents. The social currents generated by the collectivity etiologically produce modes of behavior that are distinct from the observed conduct of individuals acting alone.

PURPOSE

The aim of the research presented here is to identify and compare essential patterns of delinquency exhibited by organized gangs and spontaneously formed groups in the city of Philadelphia. The major source of data consists of all gang and group events that came to the attention of the Gang Control Unit of the Police Department of Philadelphia during the year beginning July 1, 1965 and ending June 30, 1966.

Unlike recent research, whose primary focus is upon individual gang delinquents, this study employs the collective gang event as the major unit of analysis. The few empirical studies concerned with collective delinquency focus almost entirely upon the individual characteristics of gang or group offenders. They ignore corporate characteristics depicting gangs and groups as collective entities. The few instances where the collectivity is emphasized are found in clinical studies of psychologists, psychiatrists, and sociologists. But in most of these studies, only one or two gangs or groups are the object of analysis and we attain an ideographic rather than nomothetic treatment and description of the collectivities. Clinical studies provide basic insights into critical sociopsychological dynamics among participants comprising gangs and groups, but they do not expose the essential relationships between collectivities nor their interdependence with the entire social structure.

We are concerned with descriptive data that reflect the sociocultural dynamics of the corporate phenomenon of the gang and all of its participants. Moreover, this study seeks to discover differences, if any, between two analytically distinct forms of deviant subcultures, the gang and the group. Only after gang and group events are examined thoroughly will we proceed in a subsequent article to investigate, employing a dynamic model, the characteristics of individual offender groupings.

Previous research has selected either a small sample of gangs and scrutinized them in detail or has examined the behavioral patterns governing a large number of gang offenders representative of a limited area and not of an entire city. No study has attempted to investigate systematically all gang events known to the police in a large urban area together with all their known participants. Because the data of the present research include detailed reports on all gang offenses reported to the Philadelphia Police Department for the time period covered by this analysis, it is possible to present a broad and macroscopic portrait of gang delinquency for the entire city.

The analysis will also explore characteristics or positional attributes of gang and group victims. Few studies on gang and group delinquency have examined in detail both corporate and individual characteristics of gang and group victims. Moreover, we shall explore victim-offender relationships for gang and group delinquents. This task is of special interest because it may suggest the existence of a single internecine subculture comprising offenders and victims, exhibiting homogeneous characteristics and sharing a similar normative system.

SOURCE OF DATA

The primary source of data employed in the present analysis consists of offense reports collected by the Gang Control Unit of the Philadelphia Police Department. The adequacy, representativeness, and completeness of these data may be evaluated only after we become thoroughly familiar with the particular police unit from which these reports emanate.

THE GANG CONTROL UNIT

The Juvenile Aid Division of the Philadelphia Police Department was established in 1932, known then as the Crime Prevention Unit, and consisted of two plainclothes officers and a lieutenant. Today, with approximately 200 police officers working three shifts, the Juvenile Aid Division investigates to conclusion all known delinquent events involving juveniles.[2] The Gang Control Unit, formed in 1960, is one of the many specialized squads attached to the JAD. The major objectives of the Unit are to patrol designated areas where gang activity has been in evidence and to ascertain the identity, size, and location of gangs and gang members.[3] Moreover, the Gang Control Unit gathers information con-

---

[2] An extensive and thorough discussion of the organization and duties of the JAD may be found in T. Sellin and M. E. Wolfgang, *The Measurement of Delinquency* (New York: John Wiley and Sons, Inc., 1964), Chapter 7.

[3] Memo, The Gang Control Unit, JAD, Philadelphia Police Department, January 19, 1961.

cerning possible or pending gang conflicts and investigates other criminal activities of gangs. The Unit is also ordered to counteract gang warfare through confiscation of weapons and effecting arrests. In addition, the Unit investigates to conclusion all outbreaks of violence and/or criminal actions by gang members. Finally, the Unit works closely with interested and participating citizen organizations and governmental agencies in an attempt to redirect the deviant activities of gangs into socially acceptable modes of behavior.

To accomplish these objectives, the Gang Control Unit functions as a centralized operation with activities coordinated and controlled by the headquarters unit of the Juvenile Aid Division. Teams of police in plainclothes and unmarked cars, equipped with two-way radio, patrol designated areas of known or potential gang activity. The designation of these areas is dependent upon systematic study and evaluation of intelligence reports reaching JAD officers. In addition to the two-way radio system, individual patrols are coordinated by the use of a telephone log. According to a prearranged schedule, each team is required periodically to contact the central operations room of JAD headquarters where a record of each team's whereabouts is maintained in the log.

For purposes of accurate files and reliable reference data concerning identification, number, location, membership, and general activities of organized gangs, squad members are encouraged to adhere strictly to prescribed reporting and recording procedures. An active up-to-date card file, arranged both alphabetically and by each individual gang, is kept. It contains information that includes: name, nicknames, age, race, sex, address, and gang affiliation of each gang member. Each officer of the squad also maintains a personal notebook listing gang members, their nicknames, and addresses so that gang offenders may be easily identified and apprehended. Often, unrelated nicknames mentioned in conversation with rival gang members lead to the solution of major gang offenses. Moreover, careful listings of all known gangs in the city of Philadelphia by police district, their name, estimated size, location, and places they frequent, their leaders, allies, and enemies are prepared periodically to give the officer an instantaneous and, at the same time, a comprehensive perspective of the gang situation in the city at any particular time. Also, the present status of each gang, whether it is active, sporadic, or dormant, is included in the report.[4] Another listing contains a glossary of more than

---

[4] Although the police have not rigorously operationalized these designations, nevertheless, they consider an active gang one that comes to the attention of the police at least every three months; a sporadic gang about once every six months; and a dormant gang once a year. According to police estimates, 60 percent of the gangs are active; 31 percent sporadic; and 9 percent dormant.

350 terms of gang argot. Knowledge of this lexicon facilitates verbal communication between officers and gang members that often leads to supplemental information useful for crime prevention. Additional information on recently recruited gang members, possession of weapons by gang members, rival gangs, gang hideouts, and impending gang conflicts is obtained and carefully recorded during preventive patrol and frequent checks of recreation centers, playgrounds, schools, dances, parties, and civic functions.

OFFENSE DATA

The Gang Control Unit began in 1965 to collect systematically offense and investigation reports[5] of all known delinquent acts committed by juvenile gangs and selected groups in the city of Philadelphia. The reports maintained at Gang Control Headquarters, located at 13th and Thompson Streets, are filed according to month and district of occurrence of the delinquent event.

The first phase of the present research consists of an analysis of all gang and group events, investigated by the Gang Control Unit, that occurred in the city of Philadelphia during the one-year period beginning July 1, 1965. This time period was selected for two reasons: first, the reports covering this particular time span contain recent offenses committed by gangs and groups. Our analysis will thus provide a description of the current status of delinquent collectivities. Second, beginning in 1965, more stringent and consistent recording procedures were ordered by the police department.[6] It was thought that a six-month period would provide the Gang Control Unit personnel sufficient time to adapt to the changes, thus achieving optimum standardization in reporting.

Examination of the records revealed that the Gang Control Unit investigated to conclusion 312 gang and group events. Of these, 217 were gang incidents and 95 were attributed to groups.

GANG AND GROUP EVENTS

Because this research almost entirely relies upon police definitions of gangs and groups, at least three questions must be answered. First, what

---

[5] For an evaluation of the accuracy, completeness, and representativeness of JAD offense reports and master file record card (discussed below), see Sellin and Wolfgang, op. cit., pp. 104-113.

[6] For instance, Gang Control officers were instructed to differentiate between gangs and groups in the report.

types of collectivities and aggregates correspond to police conceptions of gangs and groups? Second, what "operational" criteria are employed by the police to differentiate gang events from group events? And last, by what procedures do all or at least the vast bulk of gang events known to the Philadelphia Police Department ultimately come to the attention of the Gang Control Unit?

The Gang Control Unit places great emphasis upon the distinction between gangs and groups. Informal, unstructured interviews with randomly selected gang control personnel indicate, perhaps surprisingly, that police conceptions of each of these distinct collectivities are similar to corresponding theoretical distinctions made by sociologists.[7] The *gang* is a highly developed aggregate whose membership is relatively large. Moreover, gangs have an elaborate organization and include such differentiated roles as leaders, lieutenants, war counsellors, checkers, and runners. The gangs have names and an intense sense of corporate identify and identify with a particular circumscribed territory or "turf." Status within the gang is determined usually by a member's toughness or physical prowess, and heart or courage is the most highly valued virtue. The fact that the Gang Control Unit records for each gang its name, territory, usual hangouts, enemies, leaders, runners, and checkers and, at the same time, maintains an active file on gang members which includes their names, addresses, age, race, sex, etc., indicates that only those aggregates that exhibit the majority of these characteristics are considered gangs. In most cases, they have been known to the police and under observation for a number of years.

The *delinquent group,* on the other hand, is conceived of as a relatively small clique of youth who coalesce sporadically, without apparent reason, and spontaneously violate the law. The group has neither an elaborate differentiated organizational structure, nor a name by which it may be identified. Group members do not formally identify with a particular turf or territory. Another aspect of the group is its ephemeral character and inability to perpetuate itself, especially when exposed to external pressure. Unlike the gang, after a group has contacts with the police, their members rarely are apprehended for subsequent delinquent acts within the context of the same group. Gangs and gang members, on the other hand, despite numerous police contacts, continue to be observed and identified by the police during preventive patrols and are frequently involved in additional delinquent events.

---

[7] Especially Cohen and Short's analytical distinction between the parent male and conflict subcultures. See A. K. Cohen and J. F. Short, Jr., "Research in Delinquent Subcultures," *Journal of Social Issues,* 14 (3), 24-25 (1958).

It is the contention of this writer that the gang and group collectivities under examination are close empirical referents of the hypothesized parent male and conflict subcultures posited by Cohen and Short.[8] The *groups* under investigation are a variety of the parent male subculture described in *Delinquent Boys*.[9] Cohen and Short maintain that the parent subculture is the most common variety of delinquent subcultures in this country and that its membership consists of small groups and cliques. Contrariwise, the *gangs* identified by the police and examined in this research possess many of the theoretical characteristics and attributes attributed by Cohen and Short to the conflict subculture.

It should be emphasized that the groups employed in this study actually comprise only one variety of the parent male subculture. Group events are investigated by the Gang Control Unit only when initially they are presumed to be gang incidents[10] or when the unique resources of the Gang Control Unit are requested because of the seriousness of the incident. In the former instance, thorough investigation revealed that the offenses were not gang events. Thus, our group events are not representative of all offenses in Philadelphia by two or more juveniles acting in concert. They do represent the particular variety of the parent male subculture that most closely corresponds to, but is yet distinct from, the gang. The primary interest of this research is to examine the patterns and uniformities that govern gang delinquency and offenders. This task may be achieved by contrasting the two forms of gang and group delinquency with each other. Notions pertaining to gang delinquency will be sharpened and clarified if, in addition to what this variety of deviance is, it can be shown what it is not. We are interested only incidentally in the content and patterns pertaining to the group subculture.

Unlike group events, gang offenses comprising our quota were executed by known members of highly structured gangs who, in many cases, were obeying the orders of their leaders.

TYPES OF GANG AND GROUP EVENTS

In most instances the police officer has little difficulty in deciding whether an incident is a gang or a group event. Even the preliminary

---

[8] *Ibid.*, pp. 24-25.

[9] A. K. Cohen, *Delinquent Boys* (Glencoe, Illinois: The Free Press, 1955).

[10] An incident will be investigated by the Gang Control Unit if it appears to have the characteristics of a gang event. Offenses committed by a number of youths in areas where gangs are in evidence might have resulted from gangs and thus are referred to the Gang Control Unit. The exact procedure of how these events come to the attention of the Unit will be discussed in the text below.

investigation yields many indicators that provide a valid basis upon which the Gang Control officer may decide which type of collectivity was responsible for the delinquent event.

Gang events may be classified into four categories: (1) the multiple-purposive gang event; (2) the gang fight; (3) the single-purposive gang event; and (4) the multiple-nonpurposive gang event. In addition to defining each event type, several typical case illustrations from the Gang Control Unit will be provided so that the rationale behind the police classification will be understood.

The Multiple-Purposive Gang Event

A multiple-purposive gang event occurs when at least two gang members violate the law and it is found that the offenders acted in concert precisely because they are participants in a gang. The crucial component in these cases is the presence of an apparent gang motive. Approximately 63.2 percent of the gang incidents were multiple-purposive events.[11]

CASE 1

> Two Negroes, 15 years of age, were about to enter a private residence when eight colored youths appeared and asked them where they were from. When they replied, "Nowhere," [12] the eight offenders fired upon the two with a shotgun, striking one in the face, and the other in the hand. Police officers heard the shots and proceeded to the scene of the shooting. After sighting a number of juveniles running in various directions, they gave chase and apprehended two of the offenders. Gang Control officers were contacted and assigned the case. The interrogations that ensued revealed that tension was running high between the Angels and Cobra gangs.[13] Peace talks were held, with leaders of each gang participating, but the negotiations (as in the case of many international discussions among nations) failed to mitigate the deep-felt animosities between them. The assault followed the unsuccessful meetings. It turned out that the offenders were members of the Angels, while the victims were part of the inner circle of the Cobras.

This case is a multiple event because at least two offenders were involved. Moreover, it is purposive because the motive precipitating the assault was directly related to the tension and hostility between the gangs.

---

[11] Although approximately 81 percent of the gang events involved motives, 22.1 and 2.3 percent, respectively, were gang fights and single-purposive gang events. These cases were classified accordingly in the gang fight and single-purposive gang event categories.

[12] It is interesting to note that in over half of the total cases the same verbal sequence was as follows: first, victims were asked, "Where are you from?" After responding, "Nowhere," the assault ensued.

[13] The names of gangs, offenders, and places have all been changed to guarantee anonymity of the subjects.

Although assignment of this type of incident to the gang-event category does not depend upon the offenders' and victims' agreement with the Gang Control officers' interpretation of the facts pertaining to the event, in most cases such convergence indeed occurred.

The Gang Fight

A delinquent event is classified as a gang fight when two or more gangs, either according to prearranged plans or a chance meeting, muster their members and engage in an altercation. The Gang Control personnel assigned to patrol the area where the fight occurred almost always had prior knowledge of the participating gangs. Forty-eight incidents, or 22.1 percent of the total 217 gang events, were gang fights.

CASE 2

On 11/2/65 at 11:05 P.M. a radio message was received that "roving gangs with shotguns are in the vicinity of 9th and Lehigh Avenue." Several patrol cars arrived at that location and found a large number of boys, approximately 75, engaged in a street fight. Many juveniles were observed dropping car aerials as they fled and were taken into custody by the officers. The Gang Control Unit was assigned the case and conducted a thorough investigation. It was learned that a large number of youths representing two rival gangs, the Chiefs and the Vandals, both well-known to the police, met by chance and after each one screamed "their corner," a general fight ensued. At least two shotgun blasts and a number of pistol shots were reported by witnesses. All but one of the offenders taken into custody had prior police contacts and were known to the Gang Control Unit as members of the rival gangs.

Single-Purposive Gang Event

The single-purpose gang event is similar to its multiple counterpart except that it involves one offender. It must be demonstrated that each event assigned to this category was perpetrated by a lone youth identified by the police as a gang member, who violated the law because of his direct involvement with a gang. Five cases, or 2.3 percent of the gang events were designated to this category.[14]

---

[14] It was decided to include the five cases where only one offender participated because, as implied in the text, the definition of a gang event does not necessarily incorporate the criterion of the presence of two or more assailants. Although approximately 98 percent of the gang events were aggregate offenses (i.e., delinquent acts involving two or more offenders), this is neither a necessary nor a sufficient condition for classifying delinquent acts into the gang category. The important element is that the delinquent event occurred precisely because of the existence of a gang subculture.

CASE 3

Two youths left Philadelphia High School at approximately 3:00 P.M. and walked toward the subway. Meanwhile, they noticed another juvenile known only as Johnson approaching. Suddenly Johnson struck one of the youths, knocking him down the subway steps. The victim was taken to the hospital and upon regaining consciousness stated to the police that he could identify the offender because they attend the same school. He continued that some time ago Johnson had asked him if he belonged to the Broome Street gang and he replied he did. Johnson then stated that he (the victim) better watch out because he was a member of the 14th Streeters. The current incident was the delayed outcome of that conversation.

This incident is a single-purposive gang event because the assault was perpetrated by a single offender who was motivated by the fact that the victim was a member of a rival gang. Indeed, the offender, himself, gave this reason for the assault. Moreover, it was well-known to the police that the 14th Streeters and Broome Street gangs had been feuding for the past three months.

The Multiple-Nonpurposive Gang Event

The multiple-nonpurposive gang event occurs when two or more gang members, acting within the context of the gang, violate the law without any apparent motive. These events constitute an integral part of the everyday activities of gangs and are symptomatic of their general behavior.[15] Police will designate a multiple-nonpurposive event as a gang event only if they are reasonably certain that the youths acted in concert and expressed the collective will of the gang.[16]

CASE 4

Approximately 20 members of a gang were milling about outside a state liquor store situated in their territory. The youths, who obviously were under age, demanded that patrons purchase liquor for them. Besides

---

[15] Although these events occur frequently, arrests are rarely made. Police action, aside from dispersing the youths, usually occurs when a theft or injury ensues.

[16] The possibility of confusing gang and group events is greatest for this category. It is precisely here that group events committed by gang members might be misclassified as gang events. However, my reading of the cases plus interviews with members of the Gang Control Unit convinced me that the appropriate decision was made in all but two of the cases. These two events were excluded from the analysis. Moreover, only 28 or 12.4 percent of all gang events were in this category and, even if a few were misclassified, the effect would be negligible.

threatening patrons, they attempted to snatch a bottle of wine from a customer leaving the store. The offenders were arrested by members of the uniformed police and when it was learned that they were gang members, the Gang Control Unit was notified.

In the offense report, the Gang Control officer stated that this gang, known as the Playboys, regularly harassed patrons of the liquor store. Moreover, the youths were found frequently to be intoxicated. An arrest was warranted because the gang insisted that the liquor store was part of their turf and thus believed they had the right to threaten patrons.

Group Events

A group event, as defined in this research, is any offense involving two or more offenders that was investigated to conclusion by the Gang Control Unit, but was not a gang event. Most group events, as previously noted, were brought to the attention of the Gang Control Unit because, initially, they were presumed to be gang events. Subsequent examination revealed, however, that they were committed by small groups or cliques of juveniles.[17] It should be added that although most group events were perpetrated by nongang members, thus reducing the possibility of error due to police misclassification, four offenses, or 4.2 percent, involved one or more gang members not acting within the context of the gang. In each of these cases, the offense report clearly indicated that the incident was a group, rather than a gang, event.

CASE 5: *Group Event (Nongang Members)*

On 11/5/65 a police officer entered a hoagie shop located at 2320 West Street and observed a number of youths acting disorderly. Unable to quell the disturbance, he summoned aid, and with the arrival of additional police officers, arrested five youths. The Gang Control team assigned to the case learned that the offenders (none of whom were known gang members) had been drinking beer when an argument ensued. The group often frequented the store and used it as a "hangout," but were not organized into a gang.

The Gang Control Unit classified this case as a group, rather than a gang event, because the aggregate lacked the characteristics usually at-

---

[17] In each of the 95 group events processed by the Gang Control Unit, the offenders were acquainted with each other and acted in concert. Often, two or more offenders violate the law and are arrested even though they have had no prior relationship. For instance, three youths might be riding a bus, and a fight will ensue. Although they are strangers, all will be arrested for participating in the altercation.

tributed to a gang. Moreover, the police were unable to establish that the juveniles were organized for the purpose of theft or gang warfare.

CASE 6: *Group Event (Gang Members)*

On Monday, 12/15/65 the victim was interrogated in the receiving ward of City Hospital and stated to the assigned Gang Control officers that he was shot by a youth named Cat, stabbed by a second youth called Pebbles and beaten by a third youth known as Big John. He stated, concerning the sequence of events leading up to the incident, that he was in his living room watching television when a brick was thrown through the window, hitting his mother. He ran towards the door and observed three youths running away from the house. He gave chase and when he caught one of the offenders, he was stabbed, shot, and beaten by the group. The Gang Control Unit officers arrested the three perpetrators and a routine check revealed that they had gang affiliations. The offenders stated they assaulted the complainant because he gave chase and was about to harm one of the group. Moreover, they gave no reason for throwing the brick through the window except that they were passing by and wanted to have some fun.

CASE 7: *Group Event (Gang Members)*

The Gang Control Unit, investigating a larceny at the Williams School on 8/6/65 learned that two 16 year-old youths, one a gang member, had entered the principal's office and stolen $10.00 worth of transit tokens. The youths were arrested when they attempted to sell the tokens to a teacher.

The two events are group incidents because the offenders, despite gang affiliation, were not, as far as the police could determine, acting within the context of the gang during the commission of the delinquent event. In addition to the descriptive account indicating the type of offense, the police offense reports usually concluded with a brief, but explicit, summary statement to the effect that the incident was not a gang event but only a group assault by gang members.

THE UNIVERSE OF KNOWN GANG EVENTS

It has been suggested that the Gang Control Unit investigates to conclusion the vast majority of gang events that come to the attention of the Philadelphia Police Department. The unique methods of operation of the Gang Control Unit, plus the procedures through which the police department processes delinquent events, make this possible.

Gang events might come to the attention of the Gang Control Unit in one of five ways: routine preventive patrol, referrals by uniformed police, citizen reports, police radio, and gang member reports.

Preventive Patrol

A relatively small proportion of gang events are discovered by the Gang Control Unit during preventive patrol. Sometimes, gang fights are actually observed by police while touring an assigned area. More often gang events are discovered during routine checks of usual trouble spots such as playgrounds, hoagie shops, state liquor stores, and recreation centers. In addition, responding to the echoes of gun blasts, observing youth scattering or running away from a particular area, or confrontation with large aggregates of juveniles acting disorderly often result in the discovery of gang incidents.[18]

Police Referrals

The majority of gang events are referred to the Gang Control Unit, usually by other units and divisions within the police department. The uniformed police, due partly to the large number of police patrol cars assigned to an area, ordinarily are the first to respond to an offense. If the police observe or even suspect[19] that a gang was involved in the incident, they must and will immediately notify Gang Control headquarters. In many cases, where large groups of youths are involved, the line squad will request that the Gang Control Unit investigate the case because of their unique resources and experience in dealing with aggregates of juveniles.

Citizen Reports

Gang events are sometimes reported directly to Gang Control headquarters by interested citizens aware of the existence of the Unit.[20] A citizen might report an offense recently committed by gangs or groups. More often, the caller merely states that a gang or group of juveniles are acting disorderly and about to engage, presumably, in more serious

---

[18] This writer accompanied G.C.U. teams on field operations numerous times and witnessed many gang incidents that were either observed during preventive patrol or broadcast over police radio.

[19] The police who patrol an area are very familiar with the gangs and gang members operating in their sector. However, unlike Gang Control officers, they possess neither the investigative expertise nor the macroscopic perspective pertaining to gang activities for the entire city.

[20] Many citizens who reside in known gang areas are acquainted with the Gang Control officers assigned to their location.

violation of the law. In both instances, the Gang Control team already patrolling the area will be contacted via police radio and immediately dispatched to the location.

Gang Member Reports

The unique relationship between Gang Control personnel and gang youth provides a channel through which important facts regarding impending or completed delinquent gang events is received. Moreover, the numerous contacts and long hours spent in conversation with gang members yield information that often leads to discovery and arrest of offenders.

Police Radio

Finally, some gang events are broadcast directly over police radio to teams operating in the field. A radio message might, for instance, state "Gang fight at 32nd and Wood Street." The Gang Control Unit officers assigned to patrol the area where the event is in progress will immediately proceed to the location. If, upon arriving at the scene, the uniformed police have already made an arrest, Gang Control officers will go to the police district where the offenders are being detained and take charge of the investigation.

GANG AND GROUP EVENTS

Consistent with current subcultural theorizing, we have assumed that gang and group events in this study represent two analytically separable corporate aggregates, identifiable by distinct behavioral patterns. If this assumption is valid and if indeed variant forms of delinquent subcultures do exist, we might anticipate that this analysis of events emanating from the distinct aggregates will expose certain essential parameters that specify further the boundaries of the subculture.

Admittedly, knowledge concerning norms, values, and symbols shared by members of the subculture cannot be obtained directly from police reports. Only clinical investigations focusing upon individual or group behavior, attitudes, and aspirations can do that. Analysis of police reports will allow us, however, to observe essential empirical uniformities and sociological regularities that characterize the social structure of the subcultural collectivities. Specifically, the Philadelphia data provide an opportunity to examine similarities and differences among gang and group events with regard to the content of the offense and the aggregate characteristics of, and relationships between, offenders and victims. If the basic identification by criminological theories of variant subcultures is valid, we should expect to find appreciable differences between the gang and group subcultures on each of these dimensions. Unique patterns of delinquency should emerge that pertain to one, but not to the other, collective entity studied. Indeed, three critical *a priori* assumptions may be formulated: gang and group events differ in (1) the diversity of content of offenses; (2) the aggregate characteristics of offenders; and (3) the aggregate characteristics of victims.

The specific hypotheses that accompany the examination of each assumption will specify, based upon prior literature, the predicted directions in which we might expect the principal differences to occur.[21]

---

[21] The present research has both an enumerative and analytical aim. The enumerative purpose is to ascertain the frequency of selective characteristics pertaining to gang and group offenders. The analytical aspect is to determine the reasons "why" these selective patterns are ordered in a particular way. We are concerned with the underlying causes that generate the observed frequencies displayed by the data.

Although we have taken the entire quota of gang and group events that have come to the attention of the police during the year under study, because of our analytical interest, tests of significance would ordinarily be appropriate. [See W. E. Deming, "On the Distinction Between Enumerative and Analytic Survey," *Journal of the American Statistical Association*, 48:262 (1953), pp. 244-253, who argues that tests of significance should be applied to a quota as well as a sample because both involve sampling error. Other methodologists, however, are reluctant to use tests of significance when all cases for a specified time period are studied.]

However, due to the particular nature of this research it was decided to omit rigorous hypotheses testing. Three reasons mostly contributed to this decision.

First, this research is primarily interested in patterns of findings rather than individual comparisons. [The present discussion draws heavily upon Gerhard Lenski's comments on sampling error and statistical inference. G. Lenski, *The Religious Factor* (New York: Doubleday & Co., 1961), pp. 331-340. For similar views, see S. A. Stouffer, "Communism, Conformity and Civil Liberties," in *Sociological Research I: A Case Approach*, M. W. Riley, ed. (New York: Harcourt, Brace & World, Inc., 1963), pp. 270-275; L. Kish, "Some Statistical Problems in Research Design," *Amer. Sociol. Rev.*, 24, 335-338 (June 1959); J. K. Skipper, A. L. Guenther and G. Nass, "The Sacredness of .05: A Note Concerning the Uses of Statistical Levels of Significance in Social Science," *The American Sociologist*, 2 (1), 16-18 (February 1967).] By seeking patterns we hope to emphasize relationships among a number of variables rather than individual relationships between any two selected factors. Indeed, we wish to guard against ignoring differences which, although not significant, may be indicative of important contrasts. As Lenski argues, " . . . statisticians have long noted if one simply examines enough relationships, some are certain by virtue of the laws of probability, to prove statistically significant at some impressive level. By focusing on items out of context one can easily come to very misleading conclusions. Similarly, by ignoring the larger context it is possible to overlook a particular relationship on the grounds that it is not statistically significant, when in fact it may be socially quite significant, and, furthermore, part of a consistent pattern of findings." (Lenski, *op. cit.*, p. 333.)

Second, when consistent patterns are observed and a number of relationships are found, the probability that the pattern is due merely to sampling error is much less

It will be remembered that the group events under investigation do not comprise all aggregate offenses that come to the attention of the police. They are offenses of a kind that led the police to assume that they were gang events. We should expect, then, similarities among gang and group events to be greater than corresponding differences. Much greater differences would be expected if gang events were compared to a representative sample of group events drawn from the universe of the parent male subculture.

It is assumed that gang and group events differ in the diversity of content of offenses. One of the implicit consequences of this assumption is that gang and group juveniles, acting within the context of their respective subcultures, engage collectively in different types of delinquent events. Furthermore, evidence based upon field observations and informal study of delinquent youth suggests that organized juvenile gangs engage in conflict oriented behavior more often that do loosely integrated delinquent groups.[22] Much of the delinquency of a gang centers about the protection of a particular turf, and violence and aggression are frequently the response to those who violate its territorial boundaries. It is expected then that gangs, significantly more often than groups, commit particular offense types that embody assaultive behavior. Thus, it may be hypothesized that "Among the cases in our study a greater proportion of gang events than group events involve violence."

Table 1 contains the frequency distribution of the 312 gang and group events by Philadelphia Crime Code. The model category of offenses for both gangs and groups is aggravated assault and battery; 44 percent of all the events fall into this category. Simple assaults account for the second largest proportion of offenses, or 17[23] percent of the total

---

than the corresponding probability for any single relationship. (See, for instance, H. Zetterberg. "On Axiomatic Theories in Sociology" in *The Language of Social Research*, P. F. Lazarsfeld and M. Rosenberg, eds. (Illinois: The Free Press, 1955), p. 535). Thus, the consistent patterning of difference in the predicted direction between gangs and groups for the event and offender analysis (next article) increases our confidence in the findings above and beyond the significant level attained for any individual comparison.

Third, the present study is the first attempt to present systematically structural uniformities and patterns of behavior governing gang events and offenders for an entire urban area. The main thrust of this research, therefore, is exploratory. More rigorous hypotheses testing will come later after additional empirical data have been gathered and more precise formulations constructed.

It is in view of these facts, together with the hope of making the text more readable, that the present analysis does not subject the Philadelphia data to tests of significance.

[22] Cohen, Cloward-Ohlin, Spergel, and Yablonsky all point toward the organized or semi-integrated gang as the primary carrier of violence and conflict.

[23] In the text, percentages have usually been rounded to tenths of percent.

TABLE 1

Philadelphia Crime Code Distribution by Gang and Group Events

Philadelphia Crime Code	Gang		Group		Total	
	N	Percent	N	Percent	N	Percent
Homicide	3	1.38	1	1.05	4	1.28
Rape	—	—	—	—	—	—
Robbery	1	.46	9	9.47	10	3.21
Aggravated assault and battery	109	50.23	28	29.47	137	43.91
Burglary	2	.92	1	1.05	3	.96
Larceny	—	—	2	2.11	2	.64
Auto theft	—	—	1	1.05	1	.32
Assault	32	14.75	21	22.11	53	16.99
Forgery and Counterfeiting	—	—	—	—	—	—
Embezzlement and fraud	—	—	—	—	—	—
RSG	—	—	—	—	—	—
Weapons	28	12.90	9	9.47	37	11.86
Prostitution	—	—	—	—	—	—
Sex offenses	—	—	—	—	—	—
Narcotics	—	—	1	1.05	1	.32
Liquor law violations	—	—	—	—	—	—
Drunkenness	1	.46	—	—	1	.32
Disorderly conduct	31	14.29	15	15.79	46	14.74
Corner lounge	1	.46	1	1.05	2	.64
Vagrancy	—	—	—	—	—	—
Gambling	—	—	—	—	—	—
Trespassing	2	.92	1	1.05	3	.96
Threats	4	1.84	—	—	4	1.28
Malicious mischief	2	.92	3	3.16	5	1.60
Arson	1	.46	—	—	1	.32
Truancy	—	—	2	2.11	2	.64
Total	217	100.00	95	100.00	312	100.00

number of events. Both gangs and groups, then, engage in violent and aggressive behavior. Further examination of the data reveals that 145, or 66.4 percent, of the gang events comprise the violent offense categories of homicide, rape, aggravated assault and battery, and simple assault, compared to 50, or 52.6 percent, of the group events. None of the aggregates committed rape, but three or 1.4 percent of the gang and one or 1.1 percent of the group events involved homicide. These findings not only confirm our hypothesis that gangs engage in more violent behavior than do groups, but the data also indicate that, by far, the predominant activity of delinquent gangs centers around violence.

Examination of additional offense categories shows that a relatively high proportion of gang (31, or 14.3 percent) and group (15, or 15.8 percent) events fall into the disorderly conduct category. At the same time 12.9 and 9.5 percent of the gang and group events, respectively, involve weapons-law violations. Events in both of these offense categories could have led to violence.

Only six (2.8 percent) of the gang, and 3 (3.2 percent) of the group events involved malicious mischief and threats. None of the gang or group events fell into the sex, gambling, or liquor-law violation categories, and only one aggregate, a group, was apprehended for narcotics law violation.

A corollary of the first hypothesis states that "Among the cases in our study, group events are characterized by a greater proportion of property offenses." Further examination of the data in Table 1 reveals that 13.7 percent of the group events consist of property offenses (i.e., robbery, larceny, burglary, and auto theft), compared to only 1.4 percent for gang events. Moreover, only one of the gang events involved robbery, whereas nine, or 9.5 percent, of the group events fell into this crime category. Although all events were investigated initially by the Gang Control Unit because they appeared to have resulted from gang action, the proportion of property offenses in group events is almost ten times higher than in gang events. In fact, no gang was apprehended for the commission of larceny or auto theft. Apparently, the gang is highly specialized in its selection of offenses, while the group is relatively versatile.

The greater tendency of groups to engage in property offenses is also reflected in the amount stolen and damaged. Our data indicate (if we ignore legal categories) that 1.4 and 2.8 percent of the gang events involved theft and damage, respectively, compared to corresponding values of 11.6 and 5.3 percent for group events. Moreover, the total amount stolen and damaged is greater for groups ($320) than for gangs ($210). The mean amount stolen per event by groups and gangs are $3.37 and $1.00, respectively. Likewise, total damage by groups amount to $220 compared to $164 by gangs. The respective means are $2.32 and $.76. In general, the total amount stolen and damaged by the 312 gangs and groups is relatively low ($914), yielding a mean of $2.93. Thus, qualitatively as well as quantitatively, delinquent groups are more prone to engage in offenses involving the loss of money and property.

Seriousness Scores

The 312 events were scored individually employing the magnitude scale values developed by Sellin and Wolfgang[24] to estimate the qualitative as well as quantitative harm inflicted on the community by gangs and groups. Specifically, because a disproportionate number of gang events fall into the crimes of violence categories, it was hypothesized that "Among the cases in our study, gang events are characterized by a greater proportion of offenses with high seriousness scores." The distribution of scores presented in Table 2 reveals that 67.3 percent of the gang events fall into the seriousness category of 300 or higher. Only 47.1 percent of the group events have seriousness scores of this magnitude. Moreover, 35.9 percent of the gang events, compared to only 18.9 percent of the group events, display seriousness scores of 700 or more. The mean seriousness score for gang events is 555.1 compared to 402.6 for the group events. Apparently, our hypothesis is confirmed and, if the extent of harm

TABLE 2

Seriousness Scores for Gang and Group Events

Seriousness Score	Gang		Group		Total	
	N	Percent	N	Percent	N	Percent
1—	1	.46	3	3.15	4	1.28
2— 19	28	12.90	14	14.73	42	13.46
20— 49	5	2.30	1	1.05	6	1.92
50— 99	1	.46	—	—	1	.32
100— 199	25	11.52	24	25.26	49	15.71
200— 299	11	5.06	9	9.47	20	6.41
300— 399	20	9.21	4	4.21	24	7.69
400— 499	44	20.27	17	17.89	61	19.55
500— 699	4	1.84	5	5.26	9	2.88
700— 999	58	26.72	12	12.63	70	22.44
1,000—1,999	15	6.91	5	5.26	20	6.41
2,000—2,999	5	2.30	1	1.05	6	1.92
Unknown	—	—	—	—	—	—
Total	217	100.00	95	100.00	312	100.00

[24] See introduction to this volume.

inflicted on the community is our criterion, gangs are more inimical to society than are delinquent groups.

The finding that gang events on the average are more serious than group events, when all three of the dimensions of harm are combined, is definitely related to the injury component. Our analysis shows that 202, or 64.7 percent, of the total 312 events involved various degrees of physical injury to 248 individual victims. Of these, 181 persons were either killed or injured by gangs and 67 by groups. The data reveal that more than twice as many gang victims (79 or 43.7 percent), compared to group victims (13 or 19.4 percent), sustained injuries requiring hospitalization. Moreover, a slightly greater proportion of gang than group victims (71 or 39.2 percent and 23 or 34.3 percent, respectively) were treated and discharged. Contrariwise, more than twice as many group victims (30 or 44.8 percent), compared to gang victims (28 or 15.5 percent), sustained minor harm. The mean seriousness scores, 650.3 for gangs and 419.3 for groups, summarize these relations, and were computed solely on the basis of events where physical injury was sustained.

The proportion of events in which two or more victims sustained injury is likewise greater for gangs than groups. Nineteen percent of the gang events where injury ensued resulted in multiple victims compared to 12.3 percent of the corresponding group events. This finding may be partially explained by gang fights where several individuals are likely to be injured.

Use or Display of Weapon

Prior research [25] has shown that the use or even display of weapons is usually associated with higher seriousness scores. Because gangs inflict more serious injury on the community, we might expect the presence of weapons in a disproportionate number of gang events. It was hypothesized that "Among the cases in our study gang events are characterized by a greater proportion of offenses accompanied by the display or use of a weapon."

The data clearly indicate (Table 3) that a greater proportion of gang events were accompanied by the display or use of a weapon. In 143, or 65.9 percent, of the offenses committed by gangs, a weapon was present, compared to only 35, or 36.8 percent, of the group events. Moreover, gang offenders displayed or used a knife in 33.2 percent of their offenses compared to only 20 percent for the group. It is also significant that more than three times as many gang than group events, or 23.5 percent to 7.4 percent, respectively, displayed or used a gun. Recalling the data in

---

[25] Sellin and Wolfgang, *op. cit.*, pp. 204-205.

Table 1, a slightly higher proportion of gang (12.9 percent) than group events (9.5 percent) involved weapons law violations. The differential between gangs and groups in this offense category is only 3.4 percent although more than 29 percent of the gang events were accompanied by the use or display of weapons. This finding is interesting because it demonstrates that valid estimates regarding carrying of weapons by gangs or groups cannot be obtained from the proportion of arrests for weapons law violations. Gangs arm themselves much more often than do delinquent groups, but this is discovered only after an injury or some other loss to the community ensues.

TABLE 3

Presence and Type of Weapon Displayed by Gangs and Groups

Weapon Present	Gang		Group		Total	
	N	Percent	N	Percent	N	Percent
None	74	34.10	60	63.15	134	42.95
Knife	72	33.17	19	20.00	91	29.17
Blunt instrument	7	3.22	1	1.05	8	2.56
Gun	51	23.50	7	7.36	58	18.59
Other	13	5.99	8	8.42	21	6.73
Unknown	—	—	—	—	—	—
Total	217	100.00	95	100.00	312	100.00

Aggregative Characteristics of Offenders[26]

Since gang events consist primarily of violation of selective offense specific categories, we might expect collective characteristics of gang offenders to be less diffuse and random than the characteristics displayed by their group counterparts. Similar offense types might be incurred by offenders of a specified subpopulation who share relatively homogeneous attributes. The age, sex, and race of the offenders, together with other

[26] We use the term "aggregative" or "corporate" to refer to the collective attributes of participants in gang and group events. The primary concern here is to explore and specify further the patterns and parameters of aggregative events. Summary measurements pertaining to aggregates are appropriate for this purpose. With few exceptions, the statistics presented below reflect the combined attributes of all participants in each delinquent event. For instance, the mean prior record of all offenders participating in each event, rather than the prior criminal record of each individual offender, is presented.

variables, were examined to determine the validity of the foregoing assumptions.

Age

Table 4 presents the age distribution of gang and group offenders apprehended by the police, as well as offenders who evaded capture, but whose age was estimated by participants, victims, or witnesses of the events.[27] Of a total of 1158 offenders, 863 (or 74.3 percent) were involved in gang events and 295 (or 25.5 percent) in group events. The mean age of gang and group offenders are 16.1 and 15.8 years, respectively. Although the largest proportion of gang and group offenders are 15 to 17 years old (76.2 percent and 67.1 percent, respectively), a greater portion of group offenders fall into the younger age categories; 8.8 percent of the group offenders are 13 years or less, compared to only 3.1 percent for gangs. At the same time, 20.0 percent of the group offenders are 14 years or

TABLE 4

Age Distribution of Gang and Group Offenders

Age of Offender	Gang		Group		Total	
	N	Percent	N	Percent	N	Percent
11	2	.23	3	1.01	5	.43
12	4	.46	10	3.38	14	1.20
13	21	2.43	13	4.40	34	2.93
14	82	9.50	33	11.18	115	9.93
15	172	19.93	72	24.40	244	21.07
16	251	29.08	68	23.05	319	27.55
17	235	27.23	58	19.66	293	25.30
18 or over*	96	11.12	38	12.88	134	11.57
Unknown	—	—	—	—	—	—
Total	863	100.00	295	100.00	1158	100.00

* The vast number of adult offenders were 18 years of age. Approximately 10 percent were between 19-25 years.

[27] It was decided to display the ages of both offenders cleared by arrest and juveniles not taken into custody because in aggregate events, particularly gang incidents, when one or more youths are apprehended, they often identify the other participants. In most cases, the police had reliable information on the attributes of these youths (because most had prior police contacts). In any case, the age distribution of offenders cleared by arrest only is strikingly similar to the present distribution.

less, whereas 12.6 percent of the gang offenders fall into these age categories. Few of the gang or group offenders are adults (11.1 percent for the gang and 12.9 percent for group offenders) ; no subject belonging to either aggregation was ten years of age or younger.

Examination of the average age of offenders participating in each gang and group event reveals similar patterns. In most events (72.3 percent for gang and 62.1 percent for group events) , the average age of delinquents was between 15 to 17 years, but the average age in 14.7 percent of the group events was 14 years or less, compared to 6.0 percent in gang events. Only two, or .9 percent, of the gang events consisted of offenders whose average was 13 years, while none fell into the younger age categories.

Few gang or group events involved offenders whose average age was 18 years or older. Only 20 cases, or 6.9 percent, of the gang and 6.3 percent of the group events yielded an average age indicating that adults participated in the offense. Moreover, the average age for gang events is never greater than 19 years, nor higher than 22 years for groups.

The age differential among offenders who participated in each event was also examined.[28] It was found that, in most cases, the age differential between the youngest and oldest offender was not large. In 13.1 percent of the events, all juveniles were of the same age. At the same time, 71.9 percent of the gang and 76.8 percent of the group events showed an age differential of four years or less. The percentages would probably be higher but for the relatively large number of events in the unknown categories. Moreover, the mean age differentials for all gang and group events were 1.8 and 1.7 years, respectively. The age disparity was large enough in most cases to support the assumption of an age-graded social structure where younger offenders learn from their older counterparts. However, the differences are too small to conclude that gangs and groups are not composed of adolescent peers. Only a small number of cases out of the total 312 events (9, or 2.9 percent) had offenders who were five or more years apart in age.

Race

Current studies[29] of delinquency indicate[30] that the vast number of structured gangs in large urban areas are comprised of Negro youth or

[28] The difference in ages between the youngest and oldest offender was employed as our measure.

[29] See J. F. Short and F. L. Strodtbeck, *Group Processes and Gang Delinquency* (Chicago: *op. cit.*, Univ. of Chicago Press).

[30] The term "indicate" is appropriate because there are no systematic statistics available on the extent of gang delinquency by race. This, hopefully, is one of the tasks of this research.

other ethnic minorities. Moreover, Negroes have been found to engage in aggressive and violent behavior more often than do whites.[31] Because gang events in this research primarily fall into the crimes of violence categories, it follows that most gang members apprehended by the police are Negroes. Specifically, it was hypothesized that "Among the cases in our study a greater proportion of gang than group events involved Negro offenders." The data in Table 5 confirm this hypothesis. Exactly 211, or 97.2 percent, of the gang events compared to 91, or 74.7 percent, of the group events were perpetrated by Negro offenders. Contrariwise, only 4, or 1.8 percent, of the gang events comprised white offenders, compared to 20, or 21.1 percent, for the group offenses. Juveniles of both races participated in only one group event.

Although our findings are consistent with implications of previous research, the extremely high proportion of gang events perpetrated by Negroes nevertheless is surprising. Apparently, few white gangs in Philadelphia engage in serious enough behavior that warrants the attention of the Gang Control Unit. Furthermore, analysis of the 104 gangs responsible for the 217 gang events studied show that 100 are comprised of Negroes and only four of white youth. Unlike Thrasher's classic analysis, which revealed that the 1313 Chicago gangs during the 1920's primarily consisted of first generation white youth, contemporary gangs in Philadelphia are almost entirely a Negro phenomenon.

Sex

Unlike the analysis of race, meaningful differences among gang and group events did not emerge when sex was examined. Table 6 shows

TABLE 5

Race of Offenders in Gang and Group Events

Race of Offenders	Gang		Group		Total	
	N	Percent	N	Percent	N	Percent
Negro	211	97.24	71	74.74	282	90.38
White	4	1.84	20	21.05	24	7.69
White and Negro	—	—	1	1.05	1	.32
Unknown	2	.92	3	3.16	5	1.60
Total	217	100.00	95	100.00	312	100.00

[31] See M. E. Wolfgang and F. Ferracuti, *The Subculture of Violence* (London: Tavistock Publications Limited, 1967), pp. 152-154. Also, M. E. Wolfgang, *Crime and Race* (New York: Institute of Human Relations Press, No. 6, 1964.)

TABLE 6

Sex of Offenders in Gang and Group Events

Sex of Offender	Gang		Group		Total	
	N	Percent	N	Percent	N	Percent
Male	214	98.62	89	93.68	303	97.12
Female	—	—	2	2.11	2	.64
Male-Female	3	1.38	4	4.21	7	2.24
Total	217	100.00	95	100.00	312	100.00

that most gang and group events were committed by male offenders (98.6 percent and 93.7 percent, respectively). Only 3 or 1.4 percent of the gang events had some female participants. In contrast, 2 (or 2.1 percent) of the group events comprised female offenders only, and an additional 4 (4.2 percent) consisted of youths of both sexes. Altogether, only 14 of the gang and 9 of the group offenders were females. Apparently, both sex and race are crucial variables that differentiate delinquent from nondelinquent behavior, but race only accounts for the differences among participants in the gang and group subcultures.

Prior Record

The last offender characteristic examined was the average number of police contacts ever incurred[32] by juveniles participating in each delinquent event. The mean number of offenses per event was obtained by dividing the number of offenders apprehended by the police in each delinquent event into their total prior police contacts. It was anticipated and hypothesized "that gang members on the average would have a greater number of prior contacts" because gang events were usually more violent and serious than group events. Predictably, the data in Table 7 show that 39.8 percent of the gang events were committed by offenders who, on the average, had five or more prior police contacts, compared to only 18.6 percent of the group events in these same categories. On the other hand, only 2 or 1.2 percent, of the gang events involved juveniles with no prior delinquency contacts whereas 7, or 10 percent, of the group events were committed by first-time offenders. Perhaps the

[32] This refers, of course, to the city of Philadelphia. Police contacts elsewhere would not appear in the Philadelphia Police Department records.

TABLE 7

Average Prior Criminal Record of Offenders in Gang and Group Events

Mean Previous Record	Gang		Group		Total	
	N	Percent	N	Percent	N	Percent
None	2	1.20	7	10.00	9	3.81
1	27	16.27	16	22.86	43	18.22
2	22	13.25	13	18.57	35	14.83
3	24	14.46	8	11.43	32	13.56
4	21	12.65	11	15.71	32	13.56
5	14	8.43	4	5.71	18	7.63
6	13	7.83	3	4.29	16	6.78
7	10	6.02	—	—	10	4.24
8	7	4.22	1	1.43	8	3.39
9	6	3.61	2	2.86	8	3.39
10	8	9.82	—	—	8	3.39
11	3	1.81	1	1.43	4	1.69
12	2	1.20	2	2.86	4	1.69
13	—	—	—	—	—	—
14	—	—	—	—	—	—
15	3	1.81	—	—	3	1.27
Unknown	4	2.41	2	2.86	6	2.54
Total	166	100.00	70	100.00	236	100.00

most striking finding was that 96.1 percent[33] of all gang and group events involved at least one offender who was previously known to the police.

Residence

It has often been argued that areas of lower socioeconomic status contribute more than their share to gang delinquency.[34] At the same time, because the vast majority of Philadelphia gangs comprise Negro youth and members of this race are likely to live in areas that are disadvantaged socially and economically, it was hypothesized that "A greater proportion of gang than group offenders reside in the lower socio-economic areas of the city."

---

[33] Excluding the unknowns.

[34] See W. W. Wattenburg and J. Balistrieri, "Gang Membership and Juvenile Misconduct," *Amer. Sociol. Rev.*, December 1950, XV, p. 746; H. A. Bloch and F. T. Flynn, *Delinquency: The Juvenile Offender in America Today* (New York: Random House, 1956, p. 196; Thrasher, *op. cit.*, pp. 22-25 and Cohen, *op. cit.*, pp. 36-44).

The data on residence for gang and group offenders (Table 8) support this assertion.[35] Nearly 90 percent of the gang offenders resided in census tracts[36] where family income in 1960 was below the median of $5,783 for the city as a whole. Only 9.3 percent of the offenders came from census tracts of higher median income. Almost none of the gang members (3, or 1.1 percent) resided in areas of median income greater than $6779. Although the data do not directly demonstrate that gang offenders come from families who are economically deprived, they do, nevertheless, indicate that lower socioeconomic areas contain a plethora of conditions that generate more than their share of gang delinquency.

TABLE 8

Socioeconomic Status of Gang and Group Offenders

Residence	Gang		Group		Total	
	N	Percent	N	Percent	N	Percent
Below or $4,000	86	31.85	47	45.19	133	35.56
$4,000—$4,500	46	17.04	9	8.66	55	14.71
$4,501—$5,782	110	40.74	28	26.92	138	36.90
$5,783—$6,779	25	9.26	17	16.35	62	11.23
$6,779+	3	1.11	3	2.88	6	1.60
Total	270	100.00	104	100.00	374	100.00

[35] Analysis of offender's residence is confined to youth apprehended by the Gang Control Unit for the period July 1, 1965 to December 31, 1965. It was assumed that a six month quota of offenders would provide a sufficient and adequate number of subjects so that the conclusions derived from the results would be valid.

[36] The specified socioeconomic categories employed in this research have been found to discriminate among various classes of people in the United States. Figures of $4000 and $4500 have often been cited as the minimum income required by a family to subsist. Families with income below $4000 are considered living in poverty. The figure of $5783 equals the 1960 median income of all families and unrelated individuals who resided in the city of Philadelphia. Finally, $6779 is the money income per family in Philadelphia before taxes in 1960 and is considered the amount necessary to maintain a respectable standard of living. For a more detailed explanation of the rationale behind the selection of these specified categories of socioeconomic status, see T. Sellin and M. E. Wolfgang, *Delinquency in an Age Cohort* (to be published). Also see *Fact Book on Poverty*, Research Department, Health, Education and Welfare Council, Special Report Series No. 23, 1964; L. H. Keyserling, *Progress on Poverty*, Conference on Economic Progress, Washington, D.C., December 1964; *U.S. Census of Population 1960: Pennsylvania Detailed Characteristics*, Bureau of the Census, Final Report PC (1) 40D; *Consumer Expenditures and Income, Philadelphia, Pennsylvania, 1960-61*, U.S. Department of Labor, Bureau of Labor Statistics, BLS-Report No. 237-58, March 1964.

Approximately 48 percent of the group offenders came from the three lowest socioeconomic subsections of the city. However, almost twice as many group offenders as gang offenders (19.2 to 10.4 percent) resided in census tracts of median family income above $5,783. The high proportion of group offenders residing in the upper socioeconomic areas indicates that a configuration of factors conducive to the generation of the group rather than to the gang subculture is operating in these sectors.

In summary, analysis of aggregative characteristics of gang and group offenders reveals that gang participants are more homogeneous than their group counterparts. A greater proportion of gang than group offenders had a prior criminal record and fell into the same age, race, and sex categories.

AGGREGATIVE CHARACTERISTICS OF VICTIMS

In a recent paper,[37] Professor Wolfgang notes that little effort has been expended on the formulation of a typology of victims. Moreover, he draws attention to the paucity of rudimentary facets and surveyed facts that might provide a base for a theory of victimization. The present analysis focuses upon two forms of aggregate victimization and attempts to fill a part of the gap in this area.

A principal assumption underlying this study, noted previously, is that gang and group events differ with respect to characteristics of their victims. A further assumption may be made in light of the foregoing findings, namely, that the constellation of characteristics of gang victims is more uniform, systematic, and patterned than the corresponding constellation of their group counterparts. This assumption is logically consistent with the small but, nevertheless, growing body of literature focusing upon victim-offender relationships. The findings of these studies have demonstrated consistently that victims and offenders are quite likely to share common attributes.[38]

Age

Because greater proportions of gang events (76.2 percent) than group events (67.1 percent) fell into the average age grouping of 15-17 years, it was hypothesized that "Among the cases in our study a greater proportion of gang events involved victims in the 15-17 years of age category."

---

[37] M. E. Wolfgang, "Analytical Categories for Research on Victimization," in Kriminologische Wegzeichen, Festschrift für Hans von Hentig, Band 29 (Hamburg: Kriminalistik, 1967).

[38] For instance, see M. E. Wolfgang, Patterns of Criminal Homicide (Philadelphia: University of Pennsylvania, 1958), Chapter III.

Employing average age of victims in each event as our measure, it was found (Table 9) that 62.1 percent of the gang events fell into the 15-17 year age category compared to only 42.1 percent for group events. Moreover, only 6.2 percent of the gang events, compared to 12.3 percent of the group events had victims whose average age was 13 or below. Similar differences were observed for gang and group events in the age categories above 20 years; 12.3 percent of the group events fell into these categories, whereas 5.5 percent of the gang events had victims with a mean age above 20 years. Our observations lead to the conclusion that gang victims, at least with respect to age, are more homogeneous than their nongang counterparts.

Race

Gang victims should also display more uniform patterns with regard to race. Predictably, it was hypothesized that "Among the cases in our study, a greater proportion of gang events involved Negro victims." The existence of an overwhelmingly strong relationship between gang events

TABLE 9

Average Age of Victims in Gang and Group Events

Average Age of Victims	Gang		Group		Total	
	N	Percent	N	Percent	N	Percent
Below 10	2	1.37	—	—	2	.99
10	—	—	1	1.75	1	.50
11	2	1.37	1	1.75	3	1.49
12	—	—	2	3.51	2	.99
13	5	3.45	3	5.26	8	3.96
14	12	8.28	5	8.77	17	8.42
15	25	17.24	9	15.79	34	16.83
16	34	23.45	8	14.04	42	20.79
17	31	21.38	7	12.28	38	18.81
18	20	13.79	8	14.04	28	13.86
19	4	2.78	1	1.75	5	2.48
20	2	1.38	—	—	2	.99
21-25	4	2.76	2	3.51	6	2.97
26-30	1	.69	—	—	1	.50
30+	3	2.07	5	8.77	8	3.96
Unknown	—	—	5	8.77	5	2.48
Total	145	100.00	57	100.00	202	100.00

TABLE 10

Race of Victims in Gang and Group Events

Race of Victims	Gang		Group		Total	
	N	Percent	N	Percent	N	Percent
Negro	141	97.24	37	64.91	178	88.12
White	3	2.07	17	29.82	20	9.90
White and Negro	1	.69	—	—	1	.50
Unknown	—	—	3	5.26	3	1.49
Total	145	100.00	57	100.00	202	100.00

and Negro victims is evident from the data (Table 10) ; 97.2 percent of the gang events but only 64.9 percent of the group events had Negro victims, a differential of 32.3 percent. Contrariwise, 3 (or 2.1 percent) of the gang events involved white victims compared to 17 (or 29.8 percent) for the group. In one gang event and none of the group events, the victims included both whites and Negroes.

Sex

The hypothesis relating sex to type of event states: "Among the cases in our study a greater proportion of gang events involved male victims." Table 11 reveals that 96.6 percent of the gang events had male victims, whereas 86.0 percent of the group events were in this same category. On the other hand, 8 (or 14.0 percent) of the group events involved female victims, but only 5 (or 3.5 percent) of the gang events. As previously observed with age and race, victims of gang events are relatively more

TABLE 11

Sex of Victims in Gang and Group Events

Sex of Victims	Gang		Group		Total	
	N	Percent	N	Percent	N	Percent
Male	140	96.55	49	85.96	189	93.56
Female	3	2.07	4	7.02	7	3.47
Male-Female	2	1.38	4	7.02	6	2.97
Total	145	100.00	57	100.00	202	100.00

homogeneous when sex is examined than the assaulted in group events. It is interesting to note that in only 1 of 13 events where female victims were involved, was more than one member of that sex injured. However, in the case of males, 32 events (or 16.8 percent) had multiple victims.

Prior Criminal Record

The next hypothesis to be examined states "Among the cases in our study a greater proportion of gang events involve victims with a prior criminal record."

Examination of the data in Table 12 reveals that more than half (or 55.2 percent) of the gang events had at least one victim with a prior police contact compared to only 33.3 percent for group events. Moreover, 12 (or 8.3 percent) of the gang events had two or more victims previously apprehended by the police, whereas only 2 (or 3.5 percent) of the group events were in this category. Finally, 45.6 percent of the group events but only 18.6 percent of the gang events comprised victims not previously known to the police.

Victims in gang events not only have more police contacts than their group event counterparts but they also receive more severe police dispositions. A detailed analysis of the prior record of victims by police disposition of arrest and remedial[39] reveals that, in 19.3 percent of the gang events, the victims averaged three or more arrests, while the corresponding proportion in group events was only 8.8 percent. On the

TABLE 12

Number of Victims Displaying Prior Criminal Records for Gang and Group Events

No. of Victims with Previous Record	Gang		Group		Total	
	N	Percent	N	Percent	N	Percent
0	27	18.63	26	45.61	53	26.24
1	68	46.89	17	29.82	85	42.08
2	9	6.21	2	3.51	11	5.45
3	1	.69	0	—	1	.50
4	2	1.38	0	—	2	.99
Unknown	38	26.21	12	21.05	50	24.75
Total	145	100.00	57	100.00	202	100.00

[39] Arrest occurs when the offender is detained by the police while "remedial" means that the youth is released. Both dispositions constitute a police contact.

other hand, 19.3 percent of the gang events but only 7.0 percent of the group events involved victims with an average of three or more remedials. Apparently, selective forces are at work that predispose juveniles with serious prior delinquency records to be targets of gang violence.

Gang Affiliation

The observations that gang offenders and victims have a greater number of prior police contacts than their group counterparts might be partially related to the disproportionate number of gang victims who are members of rival gangs. The fact that 48 (or 22.1 percent) of the total 217 gang events were gang fights and an additional large proportion of gang offenses, according to reports of police and field workers, results from a desire to protect circumscribed territory from rival gangs[40] supports the assumption that participation in gangs increases the likelihood of being victimized. It was hypothesized "Among the cases in our study a greater proportion of gang events involve victims identified as having membership in gangs." It was found (Table 13) that 58.3 percent of the gang assaults had at least one victim who displayed gang membership. On the other hand, none of the group victims was a gang member. It should be emphasized that these values represent events only where victims definitely were identified as gang members. They do not indicate the number of incidents where the perpetrators thought their victims were gang members.

TABLE 13

Affiliation of Victims in Gang and Group Events

Affiliation of Victim	Gang		Group		Total	
	N	Percent	N	Percent	N	Percent
Not a Gang Member	52	35.86	56	98.25	108	53.47
Gang Member	83	58.27	—	—	83	41.09
Unknown	10	6.90	1	1.75	11	5.45
Total	145	100.00	57	100.00	202	100.00

[40] See T. M. Gannon, "Emergence of the Defensive Gang," *Federal Probation,* **30,** 44-48 (December 1966); and R. Tunley, *Kids, Crime and Chaos* (New York: Harper Bros., 1962), p. 115.

OFFENDER-VICTIM RELATIONSHIPS

The analysis thus far has disclosed that recipients of gang violence are more likely than their group counterparts to share similar, homogeneous and specified characteristics or attributes. The factors of age, race, sex, prior criminal history, and gang affiliation selectively delimit, define. and fix the gang victim's position in the social structure. The next logical point of inquiry continues with a more detailed account of additional relationships that exist between offenders and victims for both gang and group events. If selective factors are operating to predispose some and not others to fall prey to gang violence, and indeed gang victims are likely to come from particular segments of our society and share similar positional attributes, we might anticipate that unique, but essential, relationships exist between gang offender-victims that are wholly or partly absent from group offender-victims.

The hypothesis[41] to be examined asserts that "Among the cases in our study, gang events are characterized by stronger and more striking victim-offender relationships than group events." Variables to be analyzed include age, race, sex, and prior criminal history.

TABLE 14

Average Age of Offenders by Average Age of Victims for Gang and Group Events

Average Age of Offenders	Below 13		13-17		18-19		20 or More		Total	
	N	Per-cent	N	Per-cent	N	Per-cent	N	Per-cent	N	Per-cent
					Gang					
13-17	2	1.96	76	74.51	16	15.69	8	7.84	102	100.00
18-19	1	2.44	30	73.17	8	19.51	2	4.88	41	100.00
Total	3	2.10	106	74.13	24	16.78	10	6.93	143	100.00
					Group					
13-17	3	8.82	19	55.88	5	14.71	7	20.59	34	100.00
18-19	—	—	1	50.00	1	50.00	—	—	2	100.00
Total	3	8.33	20	55.56	6	16.67	7	19.44	36	100.00

[41] We have formulated one hypothesis to include all the relationships under analysis in order to avoid monotonous repetition.

Age

Inspection of the data (Table 14) reveal that in most cases where the average age of offenders was 13-17 years, 74.5 percent of the gang events, compared to only 55.9 percent of the group events had victims of this same age.[42] Moreover, in 90.2 percent of the gang events and only 70.6 percent of the group events in this same offender age category the average age of victims was between 13 to 19 years. A similar comparison cannot be made for the 18-19 age offender categories because of the extremely small number of group events (two cases). However, for gang events, 19.5 percent involved offenders and victims in the 18-19 year age category while 92.7 percent comprised victims between 17 to 19 years of age.

The age differential index (Table 15), measuring differences between offender-victim pairs in each event of nearest age,[43] shows that for 40.7 percent of the gang events, but only 26.3 percent of the group events, at least one offender and victim were of the same age. Furthermore, an increase in the age differential between any offender-victim pair to three years puts 77.2 percent of the gang events into the 0-3 years categories

---

[42] There are many ways to display data on victim-offender relationships. One method is to present the proportion of events where victims and offenders share similar attributes. With respect to race, for instance, we might show the total proportion of events where victims and offenders were of the same race. In the present analysis this would equal the proportion of events where Negro and white offenders assaulted individuals of the same race.

In this research, however, our concern primarily focuses upon comparing selective victim-offender relationships for gangs and groups. We need to examine the relative homogeneity of victim-offender relationships for gangs and groups, particularly with respect to Negro males between the ages of 13 and 17, who share a prior criminal record. Interest in these specific characteristics was stimulated by the preceding analysis focusing upon offenders and victims.

The tables presented in the text emphasize the foregoing attributes and permit easy comparison between gangs and groups. Let us suppose that equal proportions of intraracial contacts were observed for gangs and groups. Thus, 80 percent of all gang events, for instance, might have involved Negro offenders and victims and an additional 5 percent white assailants and assaulted. Contrariwise, 60 percent of the total Negro group events might have involved Negro offenders and victims and 25 percent white victims and offenders. The total intraracial relationships would equal 85 percent for both gangs and groups. Yet gang offenders displayed more homogeneous and less diffuse interrelations because the vast bulk of all gang events comprised Negro offenders and victims. We wish to emphasize these differences in order to show that gang, rather than group, events exhibit certain patterns that are shared by a single category of offenders and victims who display similar positional attributes.

[43] The difference between the offender-victim pair nearest each other in age was selected because it was assumed that any offender-victim pair of equal or approximate age constitutes an age "bond" between the assaulters and attacked regardless of the ages of the other actors participating in the event.

TABLE 15

Age Differential of Offender-Victim Pair Nearest in Age for Gang and Group Events

Age Differential: Offender and Victim	Gang		Group		Total	
	N	Percent	N	Percent	N	Percent
0	59	40.69	15	26.32	74	36.63
1	30	20.69	13	22.81	43	21.29
2	18	12.41	2	3.51	20	9.90
3	5	3.45	2	3.51	7	3.47
4	1	.69	1	1.75	2	.99
5	1	.69	1	1.75	2	.99
6	2	1.38	—	—	2	.99
7	1	.69	—	—	1	.50
8+	3	2.07	5	8.77	8	3.96
Unknown	25	17.24	18	31.57	43	21.29
Total	145	100.00	57	100.00	202	100.00

compared to 56.2 percent of the group events. Finally, in only 2.1 percent of the gang events was the disparity between the oldest and youngest offender-victim pair 8 or more years, while 8.8 percent of the group events fell into this same age differential category.

Race

Examination of offender-victim relationships by race reveals startling findings. 99.3 percent of the gang events with Negro offenders involved Negro victims only (Table 16). The proportion for group events where the attackers and the attacked were of the Negro race was 74.4 percent. Only one event, or .7 percent of all gang incidents perpetrated by Negroes, resulted in injury to white victims. On the other hand, 25.6 percent of the group events involved Negro offenders and white victims (Table 16). More interesting is that 46.2 percent of the group events perpetrated by white offenders comprised Negro victims. In the two gang events where only white offenders were involved, the victims were of the same race (Table 16). Thus, in the overwhelming majority of gang events, Negro offenders attacked Negro victims; in all gang events the offenders and recipients of violence were of the same race.

TABLE 16

Race of Offenders by Race of Victims for Gang Events and Group Events

Race of Offenders	Race of Victims					
	Negro Victims		White Victims		Total	
	N	Percent	N	Percent	N	Percent
Gang						
Negro offenders	139	99.28	1	.72	140	100.00
White offenders	—	—	2	100.00	2	100.00
Total	139	97.89	3	2.11	142 a	100.00
Group						
Negro offenders	29	74.35	10	25.64	39	100.00
White offenders	6	46.15	7	53.84	13	100.00
Total	35	67.30	17	48.57	52	100.00

a One mixed case where white and Negro victims ensued was excluded.

Sex

Victim-offender relationships for sex are as striking as the findings on race. In 98.6 percent of the gang events (Table 17), compared to 87.3 percent of the group events (Table 17), male offenders attacked persons of the same sex. Contrariwise, 2 or 1.4 percent of the gang events compared to 3 or 5.4 percent of the group events involved offenders and victims of different sex. In the three gang events, where at least one female offender participated, the recipients of violence always included a female. In contrast, the one group event of mixed sex involved a male victim, while the single group assault comprising female offenders only resulted in the injury of a female. Apparently, victim-offender relationships with regard to sex are homogeneous for all events, but more so for gangs than groups.

Prior Criminal Record

Further examination of victim-offender relationships with regard to presence or absence of a prior criminal record (Table 18) reveals that in three fourths of the gang events (75.3 percent), where information was available, offenders with prior police contacts assaulted victims already

TABLE 17

Sex of Offenders by Sex of Victims for Gang Events and Group Events

| Sex of Offender | Sex of Victims | | | | | | | |
| | Male | | Female | | Male-Female | | Total | |
	N	Percent	N	Percent	N	Percent	N	Percent
			Gang					
Male	140	98.59	2	1.41	—	—	142	100.00
Female	—	—	—	—	—	—	—	—
Male-Female	—	—	1	33.33	2	66.67	3	100.00
Total	140	96.55	3	2.07	2	6.38	145	100.00
			Group					
Male	48	87.27	3	5.45	4	7.27	55	100.00
Female	—	—	1	100.00	—	—	1	100.00
Male-Female	1	100.00	—	—	—	—	1	100.00
Total	49	85.96	4	7.02	4	7.02	57	100.00

known to the police. For group events, the corresponding proportion was only 44.0 percent, while the majority of cases (or 56.0 percent) involved attackers possessing a prior criminal record assaulting victims with no known police contacts. There were no known gang events where both the injured and offenders had no prior record, while for group events, although the number is small, only 3 offenders without a prior record attacked victims never before apprehended by the police.

In sum, the analysis of victim-offender relationships reveals that gang offenders, more frequently than their group counterparts, attack youth who share similar characteristics with respect to age, race, sex, and prior criminal record. The injured and attackers of each gang event are likely to be Negro male delinquents between the ages of 13 and 17 years.

VICTIM ATTRIBUTE PROBABILITIES

The differential probabilities that gang and group events comprise victims possessing at least one of six unique attributes indicates further the remarkable homogeneity and delimited character of the gang-victim subpopulation. It may be observed from Table 19 that the probability of

TABLE 18

Prior Criminal Record of Offenders by Prior Criminal Record of Victims for Gang Events and Group Events

Offenders Record	Victims Record				Total	
	Victims Record		Victims No Record			
	N	Percent	N	Percent	N	Percent
Gang						
Offenders Record	55	75.34	18	24.66	73	100.00
Offenders No Record	—	—	—	—	—	—
Total	55	75.34	18	24.66	73	100.00
Group						
Offenders Record	11	44.00	14	56.00	25	100.00
Offenders No Record	—	—	3	100.00	3	100.00
Total	11	39.28	17	60.71	28	100.00

a gang assaulting a victim who is either a gang member or prior offender is .74 compared to the probability of .30 for group events. Events in which victims were neither gang members nor prior delinquents, but nonetheless acquainted with the offenders, increases the probability of victimization to .78 for gangs and .54 for groups. A further addition of events involving victims with none of the aforementioned characteristics, but who were of the same age and race of the offenders increases the gang and group probabilities to .88 and .70, respectively. Moreover, the probability of gang events involving victims with one of the preceding attributes or of the same race or age of the offenders is .99, whereas the corresponding value for group events is .89. Only one gang assault ensued in which the injured had none of the six specified characteristics. The probability of such an occurrence is .01. In contrast, the probability of a group victim not sharing any of the selective characteristics is 11 times higher, or .11.

Clearly, selective processes are operating that primarily restrict gang assaults in almost 90 percent of the events to victims who are either gang members, delinquents, acquaintances of the offenders, or of the same age and race as the perpetrators. The rigid selection of victims from one of the foregoing subpopulations is thoroughly consistent with other

TABLE 19

Accumulated Probability of Victims Sharing Designated Attributes for Gang and Group Events

Probability	Gang			Group		
	N	Accumu- lated *N*	Accumu- lated Prob- ability	*N*	Accumu- lated *N*	Accumu- lated Prob- ability
Victim had prior record	80	80	.55	17	17	.30
Gang member or prior record	27	107	.74	0	17	.30
Prior relations, gang member, or prior record	6	113	.78	14	31	.54
Race and age or one of above	15	128	.88	9	40	.70
Race or one of above	14	142	.98	8	48	.84
Age or one of above	1	143	.99	3	51	.89
None of above	1	144	1.00	6	57	1.00
Unknown	1	145	1.00	—	57	1.00

patterns already noted in this research and may be explained within the general context of gang violence. Further interpretation of the victim data will be presented below where an attempt is made to integrate and synthesize the various findings of this study.

MOTIVE

The consistent regularities characterizing gang events with regard to content of offense and aggregative characteristics of offenders almost precludes an interpretation that gang activity is random and nonpurposive. Moreover, the findings that gang victims are selected primarily from specific and fixed subpopulations within the social structure identified by rigid parameters of age, race, sex, and prior delinquent history suggest that gangs are governed by a systematic rationale. The data indicate that the collectivity of the gang acts only under very special conditions. It is knowledge of these circumstances that renders inconceivable the view of gang delinquency as malicious and negativistic. On the other hand, the diffuse and relatively random patterns observed in group events are more consistent with the notion of a "purposeless" offense. Based upon these considerations it was hypothesized that, "For the cases in this study an explicit motive may be imputed to a greater proportion of gang than group events." Table 20 presents the various categories of motives[44] for the two classifications of aggregate events. The category "none" indicates that the official police report did not contain any ostensible motive or explanation for the actions of the offenders. Events were designated as "gang provoked" if they met any one of the following conditions:

1. The victim was assaulted because of his refusal to join a gang.
2. The victim was, or was thought to be, a member of a rival gang and violated the territorial rights of the assaulting gang.
3. The victim was injured as a direct result of precipitous action taken by a gang in retaliation for some previous incident.

TABLE 20

Motive of Offenders in Gang and Group Events

Motive	Gang		Group		Total	
	N	Percent	N	Percent	N	Percent
None	28	12.90	65	68.42	92	29.49
Gang provoked	168	77.47	—	—	168	53.75
Victim provoked	8	3.69	8	8.42	16	5.13
Utilitarian	—	—	14	14.74	14	4.49
Racial	—	—	2	2.11	2	.64
Not allowed in party	1	.46	—	—	1	.32
Unknown	12	5.53	6	6.31	18	5.77
Total	217	100.00	95	100.00	312	100.00

[44] The present examination of gang and group motives is rudimentary and relies upon the apparent rationale inferred from statements attributed to the police, offenders, victims, or witnesses as recorded in police reports. Furthermore, motive in its present usage refers to the ostensible reason that prompted gangs and groups to commit delinquent acts, but does not indicate the complex configuration of latent factors or subconscious determinants that might have stimulated individual offenders to violate the law in aggregate. For a detailed discussion of the difference between motive and intent and its use in Philadelphia homicide reports, see Wolfgang, *Patterns of Criminal Homicide,* pp. 187-189.

4. The victim was assaulted because he violated the exclusive sexual rights of the particular gang, that is, socialized with females residing in gang territory.

5. The victim testified in court against one of the gang members.

6. The assaulted were injured during a gang fight between two or more rival gangs.

7. The offenders hoarded or concealed weapons for an impending gang fight.

8. The offenders acted disorderly and/or trespassed while awaiting an impending gang fight.

One of two elements underlie each of the foregoing conditions. The offense resulted either from direct violation of the gang code or the gang's collective efforts to attain a specific goal (i.e., victory in the gang fight). Each of the events assigned to the "gang-provoked" category share a common motive insofar as the members of the gang acted rationally within the context of the gang. The motive is meaningful and understandable to the observer as well as to the actor. We might add that in the vast number of gang events condition (2) above was the ostensible motive triggering the attack.

The remaining categories are almost self-explanatory. "Victim-provoked" means that the recipient of violence initiated the incident by verbal or even physical intimidation of the attackers. "Utilitarian" refers to an event where the collective efforts of the gang or group were organized around illegal acquisition of an object either for its intrinsic or exchange value. Events were designated to the "racial" category when the police report clearly indicated that a racial incident, precipitated by prejudicial remarks or actions, had occurred between whites and Negroes. Finally, the category "not in party" refers to the one incident where youths were barred from a party and assaulted one of the invited guests.

The data in Table 20 reveal that 12.9 percent of the gang events compared to 68.4 percent of the group events had no apparent motive. Conversely, 81.6 percent of the gang events were triggered by a rational and observable motive. In the discussion below, we shall attempt to relate these findings to a general theory of internecine conflict.

THE INTERNECINE AND DELINQUENT GROUP SUBCULTURES

Our research provides an empirical basis for a reexamination of current formulations pertaining to gang and group delinquency. The systematic uniformities found to be governing gang and group events offer concrete guidelines for further theoretical clarification of variants of delinquency. We are, therefore, in a position to inquire, with more than *a priori* knowledge, whether current theoretical offerings do indeed fit the observed facts.

Although the Philadelphia data yield insights into group and gang delinquency, the primary focus of this study centers about the latter. Findings pertaining to the *group* subculture may be viewed as supplemental and will be used to increase our understanding of the *gang* subculture. By contrasting the latter phenomenon to the former, a more precise definition of the gang subculture may emerge.

Subcultural Variants of Delinquency

A question particularly central to the present inquiry is whether the gang and group subcultures represent different variants of juvenile delinquency. Specifically, within the framework of the empirical analysis, do gangs and groups exhibit differential patterns of delinquent behavior?

According to our analysis, differences were observed between gangs and groups with reference to the content of the delinquent event, the aggregative characteristics of offenders, and aggregative characteristics of victims. Perhaps the single systematic regularity that most effectively expresses and summarizes the many observed differences were the homogeneous patterns characterizing gangs in contrast to the relatively heterogeneous relations exhibited by groups. Almost without exception, examination of the hypotheses of this research revealed rigid regularities governing gangs as compared to more diffuse and loose patterns displayed by delinquent groups. Five selective patterns emerged that are particularly relevant to the theoretical explanation of the aggregates under study.

The five major patterns emerging from our data and distinguishing gangs and groups are:

Gang	Group
Violence	Versatility
Negro (offenders)	Negro-White (offenders)
Interspecies-specific	Extraspecies-specific
Lower class	All classes
Motive (territory)	No motive (absence of territory)

These patterns specify further parameters of gang and group behavior. The respective gang and group components give rise to two hypothetical constructs or ideal types (i.e., the internecine and delinquent group sub-cultures) that facilitate precise comparison between essential elements of the variant aggregates. The ideal types isolate and, at the same time, focus our attention upon configurations of factors useful for constructing a theory explaining variant behavioral patterns exhibited by gangs and groups.

The Internecine Subculture

The configuration of empirical uniformities exhibited by gangs, particularly interspecies-specific patterns, provides the basis for positing, inferentially, the concept of the internecine subculture.

The internecine subculture is one in which various forms of mutually assaultive and violent behavior are central activities of the participants of the subculture. It comprises offenders and victims, who perceive each other as carriers of the same form of *inter se* violence. In addition, the assaulter and the attacked fall into homogeneous social class categories, have similar histories of delinquency, and are of the same age, race, and sex. Aggression is almost entirely interspecies where the recipients of violence are potential offenders and the offenders potential victims, who display allegiance to the subculture's culturally differentiated subset of values. Indeed, it is suggested that gang members exhibit, collectively, the fears and anxieties associated with potential victimization. Further-more, participants of the internecine subculture respond in an organized manner to fears of being attacked. This collective response implies like as well as common interests; gang victimization is crystallized into a common concern. Victimization of one gang member has a diffusive communal effect on all, and efforts are mobilized within the socio-cultural context of the gang to act in concert. Gang meetings are called where participants discuss and plan common action to defend them-selves from assault. Common awareness certainly prevails and provides the integrating mechanism that unites potential victims and offenders into a single social system.

The social structure of the internecine subculture consists then of at least two primary roles: offenders and victims. Actual role participation or selectivity of which members of the subculture will assume the role of offender or victim depends upon the particular exigencies that arise. Always, however, offenders are potential victims and victims potential offenders. In the ultimate case both primary roles may be played simul-taneously by a single actor. During a gang fight, for instance, the recip-ient of violence is at once victim and offender.

The internecine subculture has its unique etiology, which cannot be clarified by current explanations of subcultural delinquency that focus exclusively on offenders. A viable theoretical explanation of gang delinquency must encompass the interacting offender-victim systems.

APPROACHING A THEORY OF INTERNECINE DELINQUENCY

The empirical findings of the present research provide the basis for a reformulation of current theories pertaining to internecine (gang) delinquency. The parameters characterizing the internecine and delinquent group subcultures imply that gang delinquency is generated by etiological processes unrelated to group subcultural delinquency. Current formulations of subcultural delinquency, particularly explanations of gang behavior, can explain adequately neither the regularities governing gang events nor the delinquent patterns exhibited by gang members.

The theoretical statements presented below result indirectly from the empirical observations of the present research and should be viewed as preliminary and tentative.

A viable theory focusing upon gang delinquency must expose, first, the essential factors that account for the genesis or emergence of the internecine subculture and, second, the critical dynamics underlying the unique patterns and uniformities exhibited by it. Solution of these problems will further our understanding of how the internecine subculture persists and maintains itself.

Specifically, a theory that fits the facts must explain why the sociocultural entity of the gang emerges in lower-class urban areas and are comprised almost entirely of Negro youth. We need to account for the relative absence of internecine strife in lower socioeconomic status areas where whites reside. In addition, the theory must explain the behavioral uniformities of the gang subsequent to its emergence. These regularities include interspecies-specific conflict, a rational motive, disproportionate territorial affinity, and patterns of gang violence. By exposing the parameters of the internecine and delinquent group subcultures, the Philadelphia analysis sharpens the questions the theory must resolve.

Emergence

Negroes residing in lower-class urban areas of the United States are not only disadvantaged socially as compared to their white counterparts, but they are also more isolated.[45] In addition to opportunity blockage

---

[45] Lyman and Scott argue in their excellent theoretical analysis of territoriality that one outstanding example of segments of society that are systematically denied free terri-

and relative inaccessibility to legitimate means, the Negro is rejected culturally, socially, and psychologically by middle-class society. Moreover, he is segregated physically and set apart from white America. More than his white lower-class counterparts, he is restricted to a limited geographical area and forced to live within a ghetto.

These factors place lower-class Negro youth in a unique situation. The involuntarily imposed barriers produce specialized symbolic systems composed of particularistic lexical and syntactical arrangements. Varying meanings of words and exclusive argots invariably emerge when groups are isolated or more or less "closed out" from the parent culture.[46] The selective symbol system hinders communication with the outside community and contributes further to ethnic stereotyping and apartness.

In the final analysis, lower-class Negro youth are not only deprived but they are also forcibly imprisoned culturally, socially, and psychologically in their immediate areas. Unable to identify with the values and norms of the dominant social system, lower-class Negro youth internalize almost exclusively the subcultural normative system of the ghetto.[47] In addition, the limited resources of their immediate geographical area are substituted for the inaccessible resources of the entire city. The neighborhood becomes their world and the sociophysical resources thereof, their property.

The sociocultural entity of the gang emerges in response to the inability of lower-class Negro youth to compete with the available resources of the city which, in turn, results in intense identification with a restricted territory. Anyone who attempts or even threatens to exploit the limited territorial resources is viewed as a predator. The emergent gang

---

tory are lower-class urban youth. They maintain, "Their homes are small, cramped, and cluttered and also serve as specialized areas of actions for adults; their meeting places are constantly under surveillance by the agents of law enforcement and social workers; and, when in clusters on the street, they are often stopped for questioning and booked "on suspicion" by the seemingly ever-present police." See S. M. Lyman and M. B. Scott, "Territoriality: A Neglected Sociological Dimension," Social Problems, 15, 236-249 (Fall 1967), especially p. 247.

[46] The underlying dynamics of how and why varying meanings of words, plus a specialized argot, emerge among subcollectivities is thoroughly discussed by Antoine Meillet in an article entitled, "How Words Change Their Meanings." See Theories of Society (Vol. II), T. Parsons, E. Shils, K. D. Naegele, and J. R. Pitts (eds.). (New York: The Free Press of Glencoe, 1961), pp. 1013-1018.

In addition, for a most excellent and perceptive analysis of the social emergence of elaborated and restricted codes consult B. Bernstein, "A Socio-Linguistic Approach to Social Learning," in Penguin Survey of the Social Sciences, 1965 (Maryland: Penguin Books, 1965), pp. 144-168.

[47] In this context Thorsten Sellin's classic, Culture Conflict and Crime (New York: Social Science Research Council, 1938) is particularly relevant.

is the structural entity that protects the territorial resources from all intruders, particularly individuals who might challenge their proprietorship.

Predictably, white lower-class juveniles do not ordinarily form structured violent gangs to the extent observed for Negro youth. Juveniles who reside in white lower-class areas, even though socially disadvantaged and economically deprived, are neither isolated from, nor totally rejected by, middle-class society. They continue to identify with the resources of the entire city, entering into competition for them. They do not share the "need" to defend their geographically limited neighborhood from competitors, and disproportionate territorial attachment does not develop.

EARLY GANGS

The hypothesized relationship between involuntary sociophysical enclosure of selective segments of the population, particularly ethnic minorities, and the emergence of gangs is supported by earlier gang studies.[48] Historically, delinquent gangs were comprised primarily of children of immigrants. Thrasher reported in his classic Chicago research that, "... the gang is largely a phenomenon of the immigrant community."[49] Moreover, he found that few gang members were foreign-born; instead, most of them were children of parents, one or both of whom were foreign-born immigrants.[50]

The nationalities of Chicago's gangs were primarily Polish (37.37 percent), Italian (25.00 percent), and Irish (18.94 percent). [51]Jewish groups were also present (5.05 percent) although Thrasher maintains that they were less numerous because of the greater organized recreational, religious, and family life exhibited by the Jewish people.[52] The author points out that emergence of gangs in the lowest socioeconomic areas may be attributed to the disorganization resulting from cultural conflict among

---

[48] This writer does not suggest that delinquent youth gangs of the twenties and thirties correspond isomorphically to current carriers of the internecine subculture. It has been noted previously that recent works emphasize differences as well as similarities among current and classical gangs. We do intend, however, to note certain comparable factors with regard to their emergence.

[49] See F. M. Thrasher, *The Gang* (Chicago: University of Chicago Press, 1927), p. 193, where he shows that 87.37 percent of the gangs comprised youth of foreign extraction; 7.3 percent were Negro gangs, and only 5.26 percent were of native white parentage.

[50] *Ibid.*, pp. 191-192.

[51] *Ibid.*, p. 193.

[52] *Ibid.*, pp. 12 and 214.

members of diverse nations and races grouped together in one area, in contact with a culture that is foreign and largely inimical to them.[53]

Approximately two decades prior to Thrasher's publication of *The Gang*, Puffer, in his study of sixty-six gangs, disclosed similar findings. He pointed out that Irish boys were especially gangy.[54] Moreover, Bolitho found that Chicago's youth as well as adult criminal gangs of the late thirties were primarily an immigrant phenomenon.[55]

The immigrants of Chicago as described by Thrasher and Bolitho, perhaps more than any other group, had the same social position as the Negro today. Like Negroes in Philadelphia or, for that matter, in any urban area of the United States, the immigrants who settled in Chicago during the 'twenties and 'thirties were socially and physically isolated. First-generation immigrant youth, ethnically and linguistically distinguishable from others, were set apart, stereotyped, and placed in a ghetto culture. Their entire life experience was confined to a specified limited area, which invariably resulted in intense identification with the particular territory and its limited physical and social resources. Delinquent gangs, then as now, emerged to repel from their territory "competitors" and others who might exploit their resources.

The emergence of delinquent gangs in Philadelphia and Chicago are apparently related to isolation and ghetto culture rather than deprivation or opportunity blockage. The Philadelphia data do not support current or classical theoretical assertions that delinquent gangs emanate directly from either antagonism between subcultural norms and the values of the parent culture or fun, glory, or profit. Instead, the gang is a structural response to threats and attempts of others to compete with and exploit what is conceived to be personal property; the limited resources of a particular territory. Gang delinquency is primarily defensive; only incidentally are actions, within the context of the gang, violations of the

---

[53] *Ibid.*, p. 220.

[54] J. A. Puffer, *The Boy and His Gang* (Boston: Houghton Mifflin Company, 1912), p. 27.

[55] W. W. Bolitho, "The Psychosis of the Gang," *Survey*, **63**, 501-506 (February 1930). Also Bolitho, "The Gangster Traumatism," *Survey*, **63**, 661-665 (March 1930).

It should be noted that Paul Furfey also studied gang behavior during the early 1920's, but did not indicate their primary nationalities. [P. H. Furfey, *The Gang Age* (New York: The Macmillan Company, 1926)]. At the same time, W. F. Whyte, although focusing upon an Italian slum community in pre-World War II years, does not employ a violent or conflict gang as his unit of analysis. Thus, Whyte's Norton Street group is not comparable to the gangs of our study. [W. F. Whyte, *Street Corner Society* (Chicago: University of Chicago Press, 1955)].

law.[56] In contrast, group delinquency is aggressive, presumably for purposes of fun, malice, or illegal acquisition of objects, and is a patent violation of the law. Gang delinquency is psychologically compatible with the set of values shared by gang members at the appropriate level of specification; group delinquency involves a direct psychological confrontation with the normative system of the parent culture. Gang delinquency is a "positive" and wholly rational response to imminent threats from their immediate environment; group delinquency is an indirect negativistic reaction, perhaps irrational or nonutilitarian, to subtle and diffusive threats of the external community. Gang and group delinquency are different forms of juvenile deviance and should be approached etiologically, as well as for purposes of treatment and prevention, from different starting points.[57]

The emergence of the internecine subculture in lower-class Negro areas only, and the group subculture in lower-class sectors where members of both races reside is consistent with the present theoretical formulation. Negro areas characterized by both opportunity blockage and isolation generate the group and internecine subcultures. Negro youth participate simultaneously in both forms of delinquency. Contrariwise, white lower socioeconomic status areas generate almost exclusively the group subculture because elements of isolation and enclosure are absent, while opportunity blockage reigns supreme. The Negro who actively engages in internecine strife is reacting to a ghetto culture. Color, not class, is the crucial element of the internecine subculture. Negro and white juveniles who participate in the delinquent group subculture presumably are responding to opportunity blockage and social disability. Relative inaccessibility to legitimate norms or conflict with the middle-class value system is perhaps crucial to the genesis of group subcultural delinquency, but it seems, at the most, only indirectly related to the emergence of the internecine subculture.[58]

---

[56] In this connection, the gang is somewhat like a nation defending its territory from aggression. See L. F. Richardson, *Statistics of Deadly Quarrels* (Pittsburgh: Boxwood Press, 1960).

[57] The purpose of this chapter is to propose an explanation of internecine delinquency. The types of action programs that would most adequately control or prevent internecine strife requires further research focusing primarily on this problem. However, it should be mentioned that if isolation rather than relative deprivation is the crucial social element producing internecine strife, *dispersal* of inhabitants of the restricted areas might be most effective. This approach contrasts sharply with current attempts to raise the socioeconomic status of underprivileged segments of the nation.

[58] This issue is only one of the contexts where cross-cultural delinquency research, particularly studies focusing upon gangs and internecine conflict, is essential. Although there is a relative paucity of cross-cultural research, the few attempts to explore aggre-

PERSISTENCE

The behavioral patterns distinguishing internecine and group delinquency may be interpreted within the general frame of reference of etiological factors contributing to their genesis. The violent patterns exhibited by the internecine subculture are related directly to defense of circumscribed territory. Moreover, gangs are stimulated to action by real or perceived threats of territorial encroachment. Because gangs neither emanate directly from opportunity blockage nor conflict with middle-class values, their primary activities do not comprise irrational nonpurposive aggression and utilitarian or nonutilitarian forms of theft. The immediate response to threats of territorial exploitation are defensive actions that invariably entail violence and a purposive and meaningful motive.

In this connection, the pattern of victimization, particularly inter-species behavior, is one of the most striking parameters of the internecine subculture. The gang defends its perceived territory and resources from others who directly challenge its authority and compete with it—rival gang

gate delinquency in foreign countries indicate the absence of the internecine subculture. The findings support the theoretical formulations of the present research that color rather than class is the essential etiological ingredient of the internecine subculture. Downes, for instance, in a section entitled, "The Non-existent Gang," reviews English studies of delinquency and argues that the delinquent group structure in England differs qualitatively from that of American urban areas insofar as the structured aggregate is the ideal type of American gang. Moreover, Downes attributes the non-existence of the conflict subculture in his country to the lack of ethnic ghettoes which subdivide urban areas of the United States. [See D. M. Downes, *The Delinquent Solution* (New York: The Free Press, 1966, pp. 116-135.)]

In addition, Fyvel and later Geis, exploring delinquent patterns exhibited by large urban youth gangs in the United States, Japan, and numerous countries of Europe (including the Soviet Union), concluded that internecine strife did not exist on such a large scale in these places as it does in the United States. [See T. R. Fyvel, *Troublemakers* (New York: Schocken Books, 1961), pp. 233-310; and G. Geis, *Juvenile Gangs,* President's Committee on Juvenile Delinquency and Youth Crime (Superintendent of Documents, U.S. Government Printing Office, Washington, D.C.), June 1965.]

Another study which has reported differences between gangs in the United States and Argentina, particularly with regard to the absence of the internecine subculture, is L. B. DeFleurs, "Delinquent Gangs in Cordoba," *Journal of Research in Crime and Delinquency,* 4, 132-141 (January 1967).

Apparently, the structured violent gang whose primary activity centers around internecine conflict appears only where ethnic minorities are isolated and excluded from the mainstream of the dominant culture. Contrariwise, delinquent aggregates emerge where opportunity blockage and poverty are prevalent.

members. Predictably, gang members assault peers who ordinarily exhibit similar and homogeneous social characteristics. The victims, as well as offenders, are usually of the same age, race, and sex. In addition, the majority of those assaulted are, like the assaulters, gang members and display a delinquency record. Aggression within the context of the gang is unlikely to be directed against adults, females, or even white youth. These individuals comprise segments of the population that ordinarily are not perceived as potential competitors of gang youth—nonpersons whose presence on the turf does not violate the gang's proprietorship.

It is not surprising that a territorial motive accompanied the majority of gang events. Segregation of Negro youth produces disproportionate attachment to a circumscribed turf.[59] Territorial attachment and neighborhood hegemony may be viewed as two of the primary organizing principles of the corporate identity shared by gang youth. Territory provides a common basis that integrates and unites the youth.

Moreover, territory defined in terms of a defended area becomes a crucial element linking the situational isolation of ghetto youth to collective violence. The concept of turf defense has been much neglected by sociologists, and no serious attempt has been made to explain its critical relationship to gang delinquency.[60]

Territory is an essential element that operationally distinguishes internecine from delinquent subcultural behavior. Furthermore, gang violence is frequently the direct outcome of protection of turf whereas this element rarely or never stimulates group delinquency. Moreover, gang delinquency is primarily defensive. Even aggressive sorties are ultimately passive or for defensive purposes. Contrariwise, group delinquency is primarily acquisitive and actively aggressive; it often consists

---

[59] See Lyman and Scott, *op. cit.*, pp. 247-248 and 245-246.

[60] There are a few exceptions. For instance, see Wolfgang and Ferracuti, *op cit.*, pp. 303-305. In contrast to the paucity of sociological interpretations of territorial encroachment, boundary creation, and defense, there are numerous biophysical explanations. For instance, Ardrey who defines territory in terms of defense states, ". . . Biology as a whole asks but one question of a territory: is it defended? Defense defines it." See R. Ardrey, *The Territorial Imperative* (New York: Atheneum, 1966), p. 210. Also consult K. Lorenz, *On Aggression* (New York: Harcourt, Brace and World, 1966).

In addition, the zoologist, David E. Davis attributes a biological motivation to street groups. He points out that "A wide variety of observations suggest that fighting for rank or territory has innate features. . . . Thus, contrary to the conclusions of some authors, it seems that aggression is heavily dependent on genetics. Probably only the means of fighting and the object of attack are learned." Moreover, he concludes that aggressive impulses exhibited by gang members ". . . have genetic components, and the survival value of group organization is real." [See D. E. Davis, "An Inquiry into the Phylogeny of Gangs," *Roots of Behavior*, E. E. Bliss, ed. (New York: Harper, 1962), pp. 316-320, especially p. 319.]

of unlawful acquisition of property through theft or violence, activities wholly unrelated to territorial defense.

The notion of territorial defense might partially explain the differential ages of initial subculturization displayed by gang and group offenders. It will be remembered that an appreciable number of youths began active participation in gangs at 14 years; the majority were between the ages of 15 and 17. The age distribution for group delinquents was more diffuse, with an appreciable representation in the younger age categories. It is suggested that "isolation sensitivity" reflected through identification with territory occurs approximately at 14 and reaches a peak between 15 and 17 years. At 18, desistance from gang activity occurs when youth enter the work force or marry. Apparently, employment and marriage tend to neutralize the intense affinity towards a limited territory. Perhaps during these transitional phases youth widen their social spheres by identifying with the resources of the entire community. Contrariwise, relative deprivation, poverty, and inaccessability to legitimate means are experienced at earlier years and are expressed through the delinquent group subcultures.

In sum, sociophysical segregation of lower-class Negro youth produces disproportionate territorial attachment which, in turn, explains other patterns exhibited by the internecine subculture. Defense of territory invariably gives rise to purposive interspecies violence. When taken together, the constellation of factors comprise essential paramenters of the internecine subculture; a social system of offenders as well as of victims. Although current subcultural formulations, grounded in notions of relative deprivation, differential opportunity systems, and system subsystems conflict, seem to explain adequately group subcultures, they cannot account entirely for internecine strife exhibited by gangs.

5

Internecine Conflict: The Offender

BERNARD COHEN

The analysis of 312 aggregate events, in the preceding chapter, revealed that gangs and groups conform to different behavioral arrangements. Gang behavior is more consistent and less diffuse than group action. Moreover, gang, in contrast to group, delinquency primarily centers about violence and rarely involves theft or damage of property. Furthermore, compared with group offenders and their victims, greater similarities appear between gang victims and offenders with respect to age, race, sex, and prior criminal record.

In this chapter, attention will be focused upon differences as well as similarities in the delinquent careers of participants in events involving gangs or groups. These events illustrate only one aspect of an individual's deviant behavior; the momentary involvement in a collectivity that frequently violates the law. Past delinquent acts attributed to a juvenile may have been isolated individual ones or done in association with collectivities other than the particular gangs or groups of this research. It is essential that we examine separately the regularities found in collective events and patterns pertaining to the entire known history of individual offenders so that a clearcut distinction is drawn between delinquent behavior in and otuside the context of the gang. Most research into gang delinquency, particularly studies that employ as the primary unit of analysis delinquent acts by individual gang youths, wholly ignore this important methodological distinction.[1]

OFFENDER DATA

For the purpose of our study, the juvenile master file record cards maintained at Central Police headquarters were obtained. The cards

---

[1] See, for instance, any of the following studies: J. F. Short and S. L. Strodtbeck, *Group Processes and Gang Delinquency* (Chicago: University of Chicago Press, 1965); G. D. Robin, "Gang Member Delinquency: Its Extent, Sequence, and Typology" *Journal of Criminal Law, Criminology and Police Science,* 55, 59-69 (March 1964); W. B. Miller, "Theft Behavior in City Gangs," in *Juvenile Gangs in Context,* M. W. Klein, ed., (Englewood Cliffs: Prentice-Hall, Inc., 1967), pp. 25-37; D. S. Cartwright and K. I. Howard,

contained the name, surname, address, birth date, father and mother's name, race, school, and church affiliation of each offender who incurred a police contact in the city of Philadelphia. Furthermore, all known offenses by a particular juvenile were listed chronologically by date of occurrence, District Complaint number, disposition by police and, in many cases, the court's disposition.

While offense reports contain information pertaining to specific delinquent events, the master card constitutes a summary of the entire delinquent career of each offender.[2] The offense reports generate data on gangs and groups as collective entities; the master cards permit analysis of similarities and differences pertaining to the criminal careers of individual gang or group offenders.

The prior delinquent history of gang and group offenders apprehended by the police from July 1, 1965 to December 31, 1965 were selected for detailed analysis. The first (January-June 1966) rather than the last six months of the year were chosen because their master file record of offenders was more likely to be available and complete. Many offender cards for subjects who incurred police contacts during 1966 were not in the master file at the time of data collection because they were being processed for more recent offenses. It should be added that six months yielded a sufficient and adequate number of subjects, so that conclusions derived from the results may be considered to be valid. The master card for each subject was located and the delinquent histories of 374 nonduplicated subjects[3]—270 gang and 104 group offenders—were studied. Together, they accumulated a total of 1847 offenses or 1458 infractions by gang members and 389 by group members.

AGE ANALYSIS: GANG AND GROUP OFFENDERS

Our method of investigation consists of a dynamic analysis which goes beyond a detailed examination of specific overall structural uniformities that distinguish individual participants of gangs from their group counterparts. The few empirical studies that have examined gang behavior employ static, rather than dynamic, models. Attributes of offenders are

---

"Multivariate Analysis of Gang Delinquencies: I Ecologic Influences," *Multivariate Behavioral Research*, 1, 321-371 (July 1966).

[2] Of course only police contacts incurred in the city of Philadelphia are recorded on the master card.

[3] Actually, 378 offenders were located—four of whom were unknown as to whether they were gang or group members. They were excluded from our gang and group analysis.

selected and studied at one point in time, while no attempt is made to analyze the developmental changes that might accompany an advance in age.

In the present study, selective patterns of deviant behavior are examined at each age, with special emphasis on the periods prior to and after 14 years. The central proposition examined asserts that the corporate sociocultural entity of the gang uniquely organizes, conditions and, to some extent, controls the behavior of its participants. Moreover, the organization of action is far from random. Rather, it conforms to specific and predictable patterns of deviant behavior. The rationale behind the major proposition results from our examination of 312 gang and group events where it was found that the parameters of each of these sociocultural entities significantly varied. Because a disproportionate number of gangs, rather than groups, engage in violence, involve a specified universe of victims, consists of a homogeneous set of offenders, and usually are triggered to action by a rational motive, we may anticipate that gang members during the period of active participation in gangs will exhibit distinct forms of delinquent behavior. Conversely, it may be assumed that prior to recruitment into gangs, gang offenders scarcely differ from their group counterparts.

CRITICAL POINTS OF SUBCULTURIZATION

This research is also interested in the critical and dynamic processes underlying the offenders' development during the crucial years of maturation. We are concerned with the temporal stages in the process of subculturization. Subculturalization may be defined as the process involving internalization of the normative system of a particular subculture. The extent of subculturalization at any specified age may be determined operationally by measuring the degree to which the actor manifests the observable behavioral characteristics usually attributed to members of the subculture under consideration.[4]

Specifically, we hope to locate the age at which gang and group offenders are likely to be least as well as most subculturized. We shall attempt to determine the approximate age at which the process of subculturization is first manifest, when internalization attains its zenith and, finally, the age of exit from the subculture.

---

[4] The Sherifs aver that a useful indicator of the presence of a norm, delinquent or otherwise is: "Observed similarities in behavior among members of one group that are not found among members of others facing similar circumstances." M. Sherif and C. W. Sherif, "Group Process and Collective Interaction in Delinquent Activities," *Journal of Research in Crime and Delinquency,* 4 (1), p. 59.

We also wish to conduct a comparative analysis into the dynamic relations governing subculturization of gang and group offenders. We shall attempt to locate the ages at which deviant behavior patterns of gang and group offenders are essentially similar, the critical point of behavioral divergence, when divergence is maximum, and the order of this divergence. We hope to establish the temporal as well as the behavioral parameters of the organized gang and the spontaneous or unstructured group in order to further our understanding of the etiological development of these collectivities.

ASSUMPTIONS

It will be remembered from the preceding chapter that only 3.1 percent of the gang offenders were 13 years of age or less at the time of their police contact for gang activity,[5] and that only 9.5 percent of the gang youths were 14 years of age, while approximately 90 percent were 15 years or older. It is justified to assume, then, that intial manifestations of gang deviance in the form of observable active participation in gangs, did not occur prior to age 14 for the vast bulk of gang delinquents apprehended in 1965. Moreover, we may assume, if the central proposition is valid, that (1) there are no appreciable differences in the delinquent careers of gang and group offenders up to and including age 13; (2) slight differences in the delinquent careers of gang and group offenders appear at age 14; and (3) there are appreciable and meaningful differences in the delinquent careers of gang and group offenders above the age of 14 years.

Should the empirical evidence support these assumptions, we shall infer that the central proposition is valid and that variation in behavioral patterns among gang and group offenders is partially due to participation in two distinct corporate entities. Moreover, it would be unlikely that personality differences alone among individual juveniles could explain the variation of behavior. We shall also be in a position to assert with more than a priori logic that the crucial element directing, controlling, and restraining the behavior of delinquent youth in aggregates is the aggregate *sui generis* and not idiosyncratic personality factors. The evidence would preclude a wholly reductionist psychological interpretation of gang behavior. Furthermore, supportive evidence will indicate that an action program aimed at the treatment or prevention of gang or group delinquency, in order to succeed, must primarily focus upon the transfor-

---

[5] See Table 4.

mation or elimination of the complex factors contributing to the emergence, growth, and persistence of the corporate entity. Individualized, psychological therapeutic programs only, tailored to specific needs of gang and group offenders, will be inefficacious if there is no indication of personality differences among the youth. Primarily, the divergent socio-cultural entities in which youth participate account for their differential delinquent patterns.

Bearing these prefatory remarks in mind, a number of specific hypotheses based upon the three assumptions, but aimed at testing the general proposition, were examined. The analysis of the data, together with the findings, is presented below.

ANALYSIS OF DATA

Content of the Offense

The analysis of aggregate events revealed that gangs, more often than groups, engage in violent behavior. Juveniles, acting within the context of the gang committed a greater proportion of violent offenses than did their group counterparts. Critical to our central proposition, however, is that all subjects prior to active participation in gangs, or primarily between the ages of 7 to 13 years,[6] be equally represented in the violent offense categories. The disproportionate number of violent offenses characterizing gang offenders must be attributable to the apparent predisposition to violence, particularly internecine conflict, subsequent to active involvement in gangs.

The following hypotheses were formulated:

1. There are no appreciable differences in the proportion of violent offenses committed by gang and group offenders in this study 13 years of age or younger.

2. A greater proportion of gang than group offenders in this study engage in violent behavior at or after age 15.

The summary data (Table 1) show the total proportion of property and violent offenses for the gang and group categories.[7] The proportion of violent offenses in the 13-and-below age category is approximately equal

---

[6] It will be remembered that only 3.1 percent of all gang offenders apprehended by the Gang Control Unit during the period covered by this study were 13 years or younger.

[7] Violent offenses include homicide, rape, aggravated assault and battery, and simple assaults. Robbery, burglary, larceny, and auto theft have been designated as property offenses.

TABLE 1

Percentage of Violent and Property Offenses Out of Total by Age for Gang and Group Offenders

Type of Offenses[a]	Age											
	13 or Below		14		15		16		17		18+	
	Gang N[b]=389	Group N=140	Gang N=237	Group N=71	Gang N=330	Group N=62	Gang N=321	Group N=78	Gang N=160	Group N=32	Gang N=18	Group N=5
Violent	7.2	5.7	10.6	7.1	21.5	11.3	21.8	7.7	39.4	12.5	27.8	—
Property	37.5	49.3	32.1	38.0	18.2	32.3	14.0	20.5	10.0	18.8	—	40.0
Total	44.7	55.0	42.7	45.1	39.7	43.6	35.8	28.2	49.4	31.3	27.8	40.0

[a] Violent offenses include homicide, rape, aggravated assault and battery, and assault and battery. Property offenses include robbery, burglary, larceny, and auto theft.

[b] N equals the total number of offenses committed by offenders in each age category.

TABLE 2

Percentage of Property and Violent Offenses Out of Total Property and Violent Offenses for Gang and Group Offenders

	Age							
	13 or Below				14			
Offense Type	Gang		Group		Gang		Group	
	N	Percent	N	Percent	N	Percent	N	Percent
Property	146	83.9	69	89.6	76	75.2	27	84.4
Violent	28	16.1	8	10.4	25	24.8	5	15.6
Total	174	100.0	77	100.0	101	100.0	32	100.0
Differential		(5.7)				(9.2)		

	Age							
	15				16			
Offense Type	Gang		Group		Gang		Group	
	N	Percent	N	Percent	N	Percent	N	Percent
Property	60	45.8	20	74.1	45	39.1	16	72.7
Violent	71	54.2	7	25.9	70	60.9	6	27.3
Total	131	100.0	27	100.0	115	100.0	22	100.0
Differential		(28.3)				(33.6)		

	Age							
	17				18+			
Offense Type	Gang		Group		Gang		Group	
	N	Percent	N	Percent	N	Percent	N	Percent
Property	16	20.3	6	75.0	—	—	2	100.0
Violent	63	79.7	2	25.0	5	100.0	—	—
Total	79	100.0	8	100.0	5	100.0	2	100.0
Differential		(54.7)				(100.0)		

for all subjects. Exactly 7.2 percent of all offenses attributed to gang offenders involve violence, compared to 5.7 percent for the group offenders, or a differential of only 1.5 percent. This extremely small difference may be easily explained by the few gang offenders ($N=7$—ages 13 or below) who were apprehended by the police in 1965. At age 14, the transitional period from individual or unorganized corporate deviance to active participation in gangs, the disparity among gang and group offenders increases slightly to 3.5 percent, still a less than meaningful difference. But at age 15, approximately twice as many gang offenses (21.5 percent) as group offenses (11.3 percent) involve violence, an absolute difference of 10.2 percent. Moreover, at ages 16 and 17, the disparity increases further and gang offenders accumulate three times as many violent offenses as their group counterparts. For instance, violent offenses by 17-year-old gang offenders account for 79 (or 39.4 percent) of the total number of violations, compared to only 8 (or 12.5 percent) for group offenders of this same age. Finally, at age 18+, 5 (or 27.8 percent) of the gang but not one of the group offenses involve violence. Although the number of offenses in the 18+ category is small and interpretation must proceed with caution, the fact that not a single violent offense was committed at this age by group offenders indicates that association in a particular corporate entity reduces the chance of exhibiting specified forms of behavior during certain phases of maturation. The similarities between gang and group offenders prior to 14 years and the sharp differences that emerge subsequent to this age constitute overwhelming evidence in support of the two hypotheses.

The percentage distributions observed for violent and property offenses might be due to an excess weighting of delinquent acts in other offense categories. Thus the proportions of property and violent offenses, with respect to the total of these two offense types only, were analyzed. The data reveal (Table 2) that there is a relatively small difference in the proportions of either property or violent offenses between gang and group offenders up to and including 13, whereas a sharp and consistent rise occurs from 14 to 18+ years. Thus the differential in the 13-or-below age category among gang and group offenders for both offense types is only 5.7 percent. The disparity increases at 14 to 9.2 percent (a value almost twice as high as the differential at 13), at 15 to 28.3 percent (more than 4½ times as high as the 13-or-below category), at 16 to 33.6 percent (or almost six times higher), at 17 to 54.7 percent (or almost ten times higher) and, finally, to a maximum 100 percent differential at age 18+. Moreover, the proportion of property offenses is always greater for group offenders than their corresponding proportion of violent infractions. At each age, the vast bulk of group offenses are property violations. On the other hand, the proportion of property to violent offenses for gang offenders is greater only up to 14 years of age. But from age 15 and above, gang offenders are much more likely to commit violent, rather than property violations. One of the major activities of gang offenders during the period of active participation in gangs, centers about violence, whereas group delinquents continue to concentrate upon property violations.

A number of interesting observations pertaining to overall behavioral patterns of aggregate delinquents are discernible from the data. First, property offenses decrease with age for both gang and group offenders. Up to age 14, the proportion of property offenses for gang and group offenders is 37.5 and 49.3 percent, respectively (Table 1). At age 17, the corresponding proportions decline to 10.0 and 18.8 percent. Conversely, violent offenses for both offender types increase with age. 7.2 and 5.7 percent, respectively, of the gang and group offenses involve violence up to or including age 13 (Table 1). The values increase to 39.4 percent for gang youth and 12.5 percent for group offenders at 17. Third, the probability of committing a property, as opposed to a violent offense, is high but, nevertheless, approximately equal for both gang and group offenders up to age 14 (.839 for gang and .896 for group, Table 2). But the probability of commission of a property, rather than a violent offense by group offenders (as opposed to gang offenders) and a violent rather than a property offense by gang offenders (as opposed to group offenders) is much higher at a later age. Thus, at 17 years, the probability of committing a violent offense by gang offenders is .797, compared to .25 for group juveniles. Contrariwise, the probability of a property offense is .75 for group offenders and only .20 for their gang counterparts. This finding is of particular import because some researchers argue that theft is the most common form of gang crime and not enough attention has been focused upon it in contemporary writing.[8] Our data clearly indicate that this assertion requires further examination.

Prior Criminal Record

The number of police contacts for each subject was studied to determine whether differences exist in the prior criminal history of gang and group offenders. If our general proposition is valid, namely, that the corporate identity shared by members of the gang conditions and shapes their behavior, we might expect that the number of police contacts for all

---

[8] W. B. Miller, "Theft Behavior in City Gangs," in *Juvenile Gangs in Context*, M. W. Klein, ed. (Englewood Cliffs: Prentice-Hall, Inc., 1967), pp. 28-30.

offenders is approximately equal prior to active involvement in the gang. In contrast, during the time period juveniles are associated with gangs, we would anticipate a disproportionate number of police contacts displayed by gang offenders.

Categories for the gang and group offenders were constructed on the basis of the age at which the subjects were apprehended by the police for their last offense during the six-month period between July 1 to December 31, 1965 (Table 3). Thus the 16-year-old category, for instance, includes the cohort of youth born either during the last six months of 1948 or in 1949 and were still 16 years of age when apprehended by the Gang Control Unit from July 1 to December 31, 1965. Because the number of offenders in the 13 or younger age categories was small, that is, only 7 for the gang and 12 for the group, all offenders up to and including age 14 were combined into one category. It will be remembered that only about 12 percent of all youth arrested for gang activity during the period covered by this study were below 14 or 14 years of age.

Two hypotheses were formulated

1. There are no appreciable differences in the mean number of police contacts for gang and group offenders in our study ages 14 years or younger.

2. Gang offenders in our study age 15 and above have a greater mean number of police contacts than group offenders in these same age categories.

Examination of the data in Table 3 reveals that for every age category above 14 years, the mean number of police contacts for gang offenders is

TABLE 3

Mean Number of Offenses per Offender by Age Cohorts for Gang and Group Offenders

	Age										
Type of Aggregate	14 or Below		15		16		17		18+		Total
	N^a	$\overline{X}$	N	$\overline{X}$	N	$\overline{X}$	N	$\overline{X}$	N	$\overline{X}$	N	$\overline{X}$
Gang	29	3.1	60	4.8	88	5.5	79	7.3	9	7.9	265[b]	5.7
Group	32	3.3	15	2.9	29	4.8	20	4.5	40	5.8	100	3.9

[a] N = Number of offenders.
[b] There were five unknown gang offenders and 4 unknown group youths.

greater than their group counterparts. At 15, gang offenders display, on the average, 4.8 police contacts, a value more than one and a half times higher than the corresponding mean of 2.9 for group offenders. Similarly, the two oldest age categories when combined (comprising the 17 and 18 year old offenders) display mean numbers of 7.4 contacts for gangs, but only 4.7 for groups. Moreover, the mean for gang offenders 15 years of age of 4.8 is even slightly higher than the combined mean (4.7) for the 17 and 18 year old group offenders despite the fact that the latter youth had an excess of at least two years exposure to the police.

On the other hand, comparison of the 14-year-old-or-less category shows almost equal means of 3.1 and 3.3 for gang and group offenders, respectively. Not only does the mean number of police contacts for gang and group offenders sharply diverge after 14 years of age, but an actual reversal of patterns ensues. Offenders who recently began active participation in the gang (the subjects up to but not including age 15 are known gang members), although similar to group delinquents, on the average, still have slightly fewer police contacts. Youth who actively participated in gangs for a relatively longer period (gang offenders ages 15 and above) have a greater mean number of police contacts in each age category. The data unquestionably indicate acceptance of the previous two hypotheses.

It might be argued that the greater mean number of police contacts displayed by gang offenders 15 years of age or older is due to a heavy "loading" of offenses incurred prior to participation in gangs or before the subject's attained age 14. Equally, one might contend that group offenders 15 years and above commit more offenses than their gang counterparts subsequent to age 14, but relatively few prior to that age. If either of these assertions is valid, we might still obtain a greater mean number of offenses for gang offenders in the 15-year-and-above age categories. The higher values would be a direct result of the disproportionate number of offenses accumulated during the juvenile's younger years prior to participation in the gang.

In order to eliminate any bias due to excessive "loadings" the age-specific mean number of contacts for all subjects was computed. Because any study employing a cross-sectional research design consists of a quota of offenders of varying ages, an exact proportion of offenders who did not attain a particular age must be excluded from the total number of offenders who were actually exposed to the risk of police contacts. For instance, data on the criminal careers of gang offenders show that 236 offenses were committed at age 14. Gang offenders apprehended by the police during the period of this study ages 13 years or less obviously could not have committed offenses at this age. Thus the age-specific mean number of offenses committed at age 14 was obtained by subtracting offenders 13 years or younger from the total number of subjects. The same procedure was followed when computing the mean for each age category, thus eliminating offenders who had not attained the particular age under analysis.

A slight revision of hypotheses is necessary:

1. Gang and group offenders in our study have approximately the same mean number of police contacts up to and including the age of 13.

2. Gang offenders in our study have a greater mean number of police contacts than group offenders after the age of 14 years.

Table 4 presents the age-specific mean number of police contacts for the subjects. Column 1 contains the number of offenders who were exposed to risk of arrest at each particular age, while column 2 shows the corresponding number of offenses committed by these same subjects.

It may be observed that for each age category up to and including 13 years, gang and group offenders have almost identical age-specific mean number of offenses. The mean values for gang offenders are .6, .4, and .6 for the 11, 12, and 13 year olds, respectively, compared to corresponding

TABLE 4

Mean Number of Offenses per Offender by Age for Gang and Group Offenders

Age	Gang			Group		
	Number of Offenders	Number of Offenses	$\overline{X}$	Number of Offenders	Number of Offenses	$\overline{X}$
11 [a]	249 [b]	143	.6	94 [b]	60	.6
12	249	88	.4	92	31	.3
13	246	158	.6	85	48	.6
14	242	236	1.0	82	68	.8
15	221	329	1.5	63	61	1.0
16	161	315	2.0	49	76	1.6
17	81	153	1.9	22	32	1.5
18+	8	15	1.9	3	3	1.0

[a] Table begins with age 11 because all gang and group offenders apprehended during the last six months of 1965 were at least 11 years of age. Thus, all youth were exposed to delinquency risk between 7 and 11 years.

[b] The detailed prior criminal history of 21 gang and 10 group offenders were unknown.

means of .6, .3, and .6 for group offenders. At age 14 (the transitional phase from general delinquency to gang deviance), the disparity among means slightly increases, although the values of 1.0 for gang and .8 for group offenders do not appreciably differ. The mean differential increases to .5 at age 15 when an average of three offenses are committed by every two gang offenders, compared to only two for an equal number of group delinquents. A differential is also observed at 16 where the mean number of offenses for gang offenders is 2.0, compared to only 1.6 for their group counterparts. The pattern continues up to age 17 and slightly increases at 18 where the mean number of offenses for each gang offender is 1.9 compared to only 1.0 for their group counterparts, or a ratio of nearly 2:1.

The data support our hypotheses and indicate that the disparity in the overall mean number of offenses among gang and group offenders is attributable to the disproportionate number of violations incurred by gang offenders subsequent to age 14. Participation in gangs increases the likelihood that juveniles will violate the law.

Not only do gang and group offenders differ with respect to the number of police contacts for all offenses after age 14, but similar differentials emerge when the mean number of contacts per offender is calculated for index events or offenses involving injury, theft, or damage. The distribution of means for gang and group offenders is exactly the same prior to and including age 14 (Table 5). The exact means from age 11 to 14 are

TABLE 5

Mean Number of Index Offenses per Offender by Age for Gang and Group Offenders

Age	Gang			Group		
	Number of Offenders	Number of Offenses	$\overline{X}$	Number of Offenders	Number of Offenses	$\overline{X}$
11	249	68	.3	94	32	.3
12	249	40	.2	92	20	.2
13	246	58	.3	85	23	.3
14	242	100	.4	82	30	.4
15	221	132	.6	63	28	.4
16	161	123	.8	49	22	.5
17	81	81	1.0	22	8	.4
18+	8	5	.6	3	4	.5
Unknown	—	1	—	—	—	—

.3, .2, .3, and .4, respectively. But, beginning with the 15-year-and-above age categories, the mean number of police contacts for gang offenders is consistently higher than their group counterparts. For instance, at 17, the mean of 1.0 for gang offenders is more than twice as high as the corresponding mean of .4 displayed by group juveniles. These findings are especially interesting because they indicate that observed differences in the criminal history of the offenders even in events where injury, theft, or damage ensued, may be attributed to active participation in gangs.

An estimate of the expected mean number of offenses per gang offender for each age category could be obtained had the subjects not gained access to any additional set of illegitimate means for law violation through active participation in gangs. If we subtract, by age-specific categories, the number of known gang events for which offenders were apprehended during the latter part of 1965, the maximum number of offenses that might not have resulted from gang action remain. This reduction of the total number of police contacts, by eliminating the number of offenders apprehended during the last six months of 1965, in effect, introduces an age-specific adjustment that compensates for the additional influence of active participation in gangs on the prior criminal record of gang offenders. The total number of offenses that remain are the estimated number of police contacts we would expect had gang offenders desisted from gang activity.

We are asserting that even if it were possible to eliminate entirely the dysfunctional influence of the sociocultural entity of the gang, gang offenders would have, nevertheless, an approximately equal number of police contacts at each age as group offenders. If the empirical data support this assertion, we will have some indication from a societal point of view of the injurious effects of the gang, per se, on the community and the individual juvenile offender. At the same time, corroborative evidence will show that dissolution of the gang would only tend to reduce, but not entirely efface, the delinquency rate displayed by the gang members.

Specifically, we may formulate the hypothesis that "Among gang and group offenders in our study there are no appreciable differences in the mean number of police contacts after all known effects resulting from gang activity have been eliminated." We expect, of course, that the mean number of contacts below 14 will remain almost the same because few gang offenses occur at this age. Any change in values should appear primarily in those age categories 15 years and above.

Table 6 presents the age-specific mean number of police contacts per gang offender after the effect of known gang events has been eliminated (column 6). Column 4 displays the total known number of offenses ever

TABLE 6

Distributions of Mean Number of Offenses per Offender by Age Including and Excluding Known Gang Events for Gang and Group Offenders

				Column			
(1)	(2)	(3)	(4)	(5)	(6)	(7)	(8)
Age	Number of Offenses	Number arrested in 1965 for Gang Events	Number of Offenses Excluding Gang Events (2) − (3)	Number of Offenders	Mean Number of Offenses per Gang Offender Excluding Gang Events	Mean Number of Offenses per Gang Offender—All Events	Mean Number of Offenses per Group Offender
11	143	—	143	249	.6	.6	.6
12	88	3	85	249	.3	.4	.3
13	158	4	154	246	.6	.6	.6
14	236	21	215	242	.9	1.0	.8
15	329	60	269	221	1.2	1.5	1.0
16	315	80	235	161	1.5	2.0	1.6
17	153	73	80	81	1.0	1.9	1.5
18+	15	8	7	8	.9	1.9	1.0

incurred by all gang offenders after gang events for which delinquents were apprehended during the last six months of 1965 have been eliminated.[9] A comparison of the two sets of age-specific means for gang offenders (before and after exclusion of gang events) reveals (columns 6 and 7) that the average number of offenses per offender is substantially reduced in each age category 15 years and above, whereas no appreciable differences occur in the distribution of means for ages 11, 12, and 13 years. At 17, for instance, the mean number of contacts for all events is 1.9, but the value sharply decreases to 1.0 when known gang offenses are excluded.

Further comparison between the reduced means for gang offenders and corresponding values displayed by their group counterparts (columns 6 and 8) yield more interesting findings. No longer are the mean number of contacts after age 14 greater for gang than group members. Inspection reveals that the distribution of means is strikingly similar. Moreover, when we compensate for individual comparison of unequal weight by standardizing on the age factor in the 15 to 18+ year age categories the mean of 1.3 obtained for the gang offenders is exactly equal to the corresponding group mean (1.3). In effect, we determined the number of offenses that the 15 to 18+ year old gang offenders would have committed if they had the same age distribution as the group offenders.

The implication of these findings will be discussed below, but it might be noted briefly that once the influence of gang events is neutralized, gang and group offenders display similar prior criminal records. We may infer that active gang participation accounts only for a selective part of the offender's deviant behavior, whereas the remaining and probably more numerous activities arise from the same forces that predispose most delinquent lower class youth to violate the law. Even in the absence of structured gangs, youth still have access to the illegitimate means structure of spontaneously formed groups.

Seriousness of Offenses

Examination of the prior criminal histories of gang and group offenders revealed that gang offenders are more often apprehended by the police than their group counterparts. The frequency of offense reflects merely the quantitative dimension of seriousness of delinquent behavior. A more precise measure of community harm must take into account the qualitative dimension of the delinquent event as well. The seriousness scores for nonindex and index events developed in *The Measurement of*

---

[9] Of course, an additional unknown number of police contacts might have involved gang incidents. But, in any case, this would further reduce the mean number of contacts per gang offender.

Delinquency[10] enables the researcher to compare the total injury in-flicted on the community by gang and group offenders at each age. Consistent with our central proposition is the assumption that no meaningful differences exist among gang and group offenders in the seriousness of delinquent behavior prior to active participation in gangs. Conversely, appreciable differences are anticipated from the time the offender is socialized into the gang structure.

Specifically, the hypotheses to be tested state:

1. The mean seriousness scores of delinquent events for gang and group offenders are approximately equal up to and including 13 years of age.

2. Gang events in our study have higher mean seriousness scores than group events after the age of 14 years.

Analysis of the data (Table 7) reveal that the mean seriousness score for gang offenses, in the 13-year-or-below age category, of 125.8 does not differ appreciably from the corresponding mean seriousness score of 119.6 for group offenses. Moreover, at age 14, group offenders display a higher mean (176.8) than the corresponding score for gang youth (144.5). The overall means for all categories 14 years and below are 132.9 for gang offenses and 138.8 for group offenses. Thus, for the period prior

---

[10] See introduction to this volume.

Admittedly the only way to determine with exactitude the precise number of non-index and index events together with their seriousness scores is to examine each of the 1847 offense reports corresponding to the delinquent acts incurred by the 374 offenders. However, the task of collecting these data was beyond the resources available to this writer. Only the 312 gang and group events analyzed in the preceding article were actually scrutinized and scored. Instead, in the present article, certain selective offense categories were assumed to be index events. However, the selection was not arbitrary. A mammoth study currently in progress entitled *Delinquency in an Age Cohort*, by T. Sellin and M. E. Wolfgang, examined approximately 10,000 offenses committed by juveniles residing in Philadelphia. It was learned that the vast bulk of offenses designated under the legal rubrics of homicide, rape, robbery, aggravated assault and battery, burglary, larceny, auto-theft, assault, indecent assault, and arson involved one or more components of injury, theft, or damage. These offense types were classified as index events for research purposes in the present article.

The actual values or seriousness scores applied to each of the aforementioned crime code classifications are based upon "mean cluster scores" derived from these offense types in the study, *Delinquency in an Age Cohort*. The mean seriousness score for each of the offense types committed by 3475 delinquents was computed as an indication of the average seriousness of these offenses. Each offense incurred by the 374 offenders was assigned the appropriate "mean cluster score." The scores were: homicide (2430), rape (839), robbery (298), aggravated assault and battery (604), burglary (254), larceny (158), auto-theft (263), assault (210), indecent assault (170), arson (499), disorderly conduct (48), forgery and counterfeiting (179), malicious mischief (124), and threats (200).

TABLE 7

Mean Seriousness Scores by Age for Gang and Group Offenses

Type of Aggregate	Age													
	13 or Below		14		15		16		17		18+		Total	
	N	$\overline{X}$	N	$\overline{X}$	N	$\overline{X}$	N	$\overline{X}$	N	$\overline{X}$	N	$\overline{X}$	N	$\overline{X}$
Gang	389	125.77	237	144.49	330	201.22	321	223.02	160	369.40	18	351.22	1455 [a]	196.97
Group	140	119.55	71	176.75	62	172.22	78	177.26	32	194.19	5	203.90	388 [a]	157.28

[a] Seriousness score for three gang and one group offenses were unknown.

to active participation in gangs, group offenses are slightly more serious than delinquent acts attributed to gang offenders.

The effect of active gang involvement is clearly observed in the patterns of seriousness beyond age 14. At 15 the disparity among means for gang $(\overline{X} = 201.2)$ and group $(\overline{X} = 172.2)$ offenders is 29.0. The differential increases sharply with continued gang participation and, at 16, equals 45.8; at 17, 175.2. A slight decrease occurs at 18 where means of 351.2 and 203.9 for gang and group offenses, respectively, generate an absolute difference of 147.3.

In sum, the observations that, prior to and including age 14, the overall mean seriousness score for group offenses was 4.2 percent greater than gang offenses but, at ages 17 and 18, the trend was reversed and the seriousness of gang offenses was 88.3 percent greater than group acts indicates that an increase in seriousness of delinquency coincides with active gang participation. Mutually assaultive behavior, within the context of the internecine subculture, apparently accounts for the increase in average seriousness scores exhibited by gang offenders.

The empirical evidence regarding the relationship between seriousness scores of delinquent events and gang and group offenders is consistent with previously observed patterns when offense type by Philadelphia Crime Code and mean number of police contacts were examined. Moreover, the scores comprise the most rigorous and sophisticated composite index yet developed that accurately and precisely measures the number and seriousness of delinquent events involving components of injury, theft, and damage. The 374 subjects under investigation manifest homogeneous patterns up to and including age 13, while appreciable differentials are observed between 15 to 18+ years. The divergence in patterns of delinquent behavior always corresponds to the period when juveniles begin active participation in structured gangs.

The overall findings regarding the dimensions of gang and group offenders and the confirmation of each of the specified hypotheses constitute overwhelming evidence in support of our central thesis. The gang apparently exerts a strong influence over its members and, at the same time, conditions and controls the patterns of deviant behavior exhibited by them.

Onset of Delinquency

The research thus far has focused upon differential delinquent behavioral patterns emanating from participation by juveniles, in two specified and distinct deviant sociocultural entities—the structured gang and the spontaneously formed group. It was observed that from the time juveniles become actively involved in gangs, usually at 15 years of age, they are more likely than group offenders to engage in violent behavior and accumulate a greater number of infractions that are more serious insofar as harm to the community is concerned. It has been suggested by our statistical analysis that the crucial etiological element primarily accounting for this change of behavior is membership in two divergent sociocultural corporate entities, rather than personality development accompanying the aging process. This is to say that the corporate entity of the gang shapes and constrains the actions of its members.

It might be argued that the violent and more serious delinquent acts characterizing gang offenders during the later years of adolescence may be partially attributed to an earlier age of onset of delinquency and not only to participation in highly structured aggregates. Past research indicates that the earlier juveniles initiate their delinquent careers, the more likely are they to commit serious delinquent acts at a later age. The findings, together with the paucity of data pertaining to a detailed analysis of onset of delinquency by specific offense types for juvenile delinquents in general and gang offenders in particular, stimulated an intensive inquiry of the ages at which the 374 subjects committed various infractions for the first time.

The following hypothesis was formulated: "Among gang and group offenders there are no appreciable differences in the age of onset of delinquency for various offense types." We have purposely constructed the hypothesis, carefully avoiding reference to any specific type of offense. Our interest focuses upon whether differences exist among gang and group offenders regarding onset of delinquency for various selective offense types and, to avoid repetition, the more general hypothesis has been formulated.

The data in Table 8 display the mean ages of onset of delinquency by various offense categories and facilitate an overall comparison between gang and group offenders. In general, differences among gang and group offenders for each classification are too small to be meaningful. The mean values range from a low age of onset of 12.7 by group offenders for runaway to a high of 14.1 by the gang juveniles for truancy. Mean onset of delinquency for all offenses is 13.2 and 13.5 years, respectively, for the gang and group offenders. The greatest disparity between gang and group offenders occurs for the offense category of runaway where the mean age of onset for gang offenders is 13.8, compared to a corresponding value of 12.7 for their group counterparts. Perhaps the differential of slightly more than one year can be explained partially by the constraining force gangs impose on its members. Finally, whereas the mean age of onset for

TABLE 8

Mean Age of Onset of Delinquency by Gang and Group Offenders for Various Offense Types

Mean Age of Onset for Various Offense Types	Gang		Group		Total	
	N	$\overline{X}$	N	$\overline{X}$	N	$\overline{X}$
All offenses	270	13.2	104	13.5	374	13.3
Nonindex offenses	241	13.6	87	13.9	328	13.7
Index offenses	195	13.8	54	13.1	249	13.6
Curfew	80	13.5	19	12.8	99	13.4
Truancy	92	14.1	20	13.4	112	14.0
Runaway	21	13.8	7	12.7	28	13.5

all offenses and nonindex events is somewhat earlier for gang than for group offenders, the nongang juveniles are slightly younger at age of commission of the first index event and three juvenile status offenses.

The approximately equal mean values observed when age of onset of delinquency for all subjects is examined is strong evidence in support of the hypothesis that there are, indeed, no appreciable differences among gang and group offenders regarding the age at which they initially violate the law.

THE INTERNECINE SUBCULTURE AND THE INDIVIDUAL OFFENDER

The age-specific analysis of selective factors pertaining to gang and group members furthers our understanding of the dynamic relationship between the internecine subculture and the individual offender. The findings confirm the three general hypotheses predicting climaxes in delinquent behavioral patterns of gang and group youth. Specifically, it was hypothesized that no appreciable differences existed in the delinquent careers of gang and group offenders up to and including age 13; at 14, slight differences would appear and at 15 and beyond, these differentials would be maximized. Moreover, it was argued that if the hypotheses were supported by the empirical data, the hypothesized proposition linking the internecine subculture to the offender would be justified. Essentially, the proposition stated that the corporate sociocultural entity of the gang uniquely organizes and, to some extent, controls the behavior of its participants.

The striking similarities in delinquent patterns among gang and group offenders up to and including age 13, together with the marked differences that appeared from 15 years and beyond, reflect the powerful influence that the gang exerts over its participants. It will be remembered that from 15 to 17 years, gang youth committed a disproportionate number of violent offenses that were more serious than their group counterparts. Membership in the internecine subculture definitely increases the likelihood of exhibiting mutually assaultive behavior.

Examination of the age of onset of delinquency for various offense types revealed that earlier commission of first offense could not account for divergent delinquent patterns among gang and group offenders. The age at which juveniles incurred their first police contact regardless of offense type was approximately equal for gang and group offenders. In addition to age of onset of delinquency, the present study emphasized the period when juveniles began active participation in divergent subcultures as yet another climax in the delinquent careers of gang members.

It would be hazardous to assume, in view of the empirical evidence generated by the present research, that personality differences alone accounted for variant behavioral patterns exhibited by gang and group offenders. The current status of psychological theorization has not yet offered an interpretation, grounded in a systematic and ordered body of data, that explains adequately why these differences, conveniently latent up to age 14, become manifest at 15 years and beyond. Psychogenic influences alone cannot account for the selective internecine patterns displayed by gang youth. The findings that no appreciable differences in behavioral patterns appeared up to and including 13 years but did emerge precisely at the time juveniles participate actively in gangs provide the logical nexus linking the social structure of the gang to differences in observed behavior among gang and group offenders.

SYMBIOTIC SUBCULTURAL PARTICIPATION

The increased criminality reflected in the greater number and more serious offenses exhibited by gang offenders at age 15 and beyond may be attributed partially to differential accessibility to illegitimate means of two subcultures. Gang offenders participate symbiotically in both the internecine and delinquent group subculture. Differential accessibility to two delinquent normative systems provides greater opportunity for expression of deviant behavior. This explanation of delinquency is supported by the finding that an appreciable number of offenses committed by gang members at age 15 and beyond involve delinquent acts likely not incurred within the context of the gang. Gang members neither engage exclusively in internecine conflict nor do they desist automatically from delinquent group behavior subsequent to active gang participation. The relatively large proportion of nonviolent offenses incurred after 14 years was probably individual or group acts committed outside the gang context. We know from the analysis of the events in the preceding chapter that only a small proportion of gang infractions consists of nonviolent offense types. In addition, it has been demonstrated that when all known offenses incurred by gang members within the setting of the gang are controlled statistically, gang and group offenders exhibit on the average an approximately equal number of delinquent acts. The present research suggests that gang offenders within the context of the gang engage primarily in internecine conflict but that, in addition, they commit a variety of delinquent acts resulting from participation in the delinquent group subculture.

The notion of symbiotic access to differential illegitimate opportunity systems or variant deviant subcultures raises both theoretical and methodological problems. The theoretical implications suggest that variant forms of delinquency have etiological bases that are analytically separable. The primary factor to variant forms of delinquency is that all involve violations of the legal code. The observation that youths exhibit simultaneously behavioral acts emanating from two (or perhaps many) variants of subcultural deviance does not vitiate the separability of their content. Clearly delinquent youths attend school, are family members, eat, sleep, play and engage in numerous other nondelinquent activities.[11] Yet most theorists do not lump these "action" spheres together with deviant acts, offering one explanation for all behavior. Moreover, other forms of social deviance such as mental illness, alcoholism, drug addiction, failure in school, etc., can neither be explained nor treated as specifications of juvenile delinquency. A single grand theory aimed at the explanation of gang, group, and additional variants of delinquency is as unacceptable as a generic theory encompassing delinquency, mental illness, school dropouts, homosexuality, and religious fanaticism. Instead, gang and group delinquency, behavior that is officially and legally identified are socially distinguishable forms of deviance that must be explained *sui generis*.

The theoretical distinction between gang and group subcultures raises

---

[11] Indeed, delinquents spend more time in nondelinquent than delinquent activities. See J. F. Short, "Social Structure and Group Processes in Explanation of Gang Delinquency," *Problems of Youth*, M. Sherif and C. W. Sherif, eds. (Chicago: Aldine Publishing Company, 1965), pp. 155-188.

a methodological problem often ignored by students of gang delinquency. If, as may be inferred from our statistical analysis, internecine and group subcultural delinquency are variant forms of deviance, then research studies, focusing upon gang behavior, that fail to distinguish methodologically as well as analytically among various components comprising the entire criminal career of delinquent gang youth will be confounded and biased. Gang members accumulate a significant number of offenses prior to entrance in the internecine subculture. Moreover, subsequent to active gang participation, juveniles commit delinquent acts within the structure of the group subculture. Although incurred by gang members, these delinquent acts are not related directly to the gang context. Studies reporting delinquent patterns of gang members, based upon the entire delinquent history of the subjects, invariably confuse internecine gang conflict with other unrelated forms of delinquency. Rejection or acceptance of research hypotheses and theoretical propositions pertaining to the delinquent gang subculture on the basis of empirical results obtained in this manner is not justifiable. Research designs should be constructed that separate, first, various subcultural delinquent events from each other and, second, individual delinquent behavior within and without the context of the gang, particularly when the offender is employed as the unit of analysis.

DYNAMICS OF SUBCULTURIZATION

A primary concern of the present research is to determine various critical points in the process of subculturization. At what ages are gang and group offenders most and least subculturized? When do gang and group members initially enter the subculture? And at what age is exit from the subculture likely to occur?

These questions are more than theoretically significant. Not only do we wish to establish the temporal parameters of variant subcultural collectivities, but we also hope to locate possible critical points of intervention for prevention and control of gang and group delinquency.

Evidence relating to various critical points in the process of subculturization emerged from both the event[12] and offender analyses. Examination of the age distribution of gang and group offenders apprehended during the period covered by this study revealed that few gang members 13 years or below (approximately 3 percent) incurred police contacts for delinquent gang activities. If the age at which juveniles

_____
[12] See the preceding chapter.

first exhibit the unique behavioral patterns of gang delinquency is a valid measure of entrance into the subculture, then initial subculturization occurs for a small proportion of youth (about 10 percent) at 14. The process of subculturization continues at 15 and is reflected by the additional 20 percent of the juveniles who were arrested for delinquent gang activity. Furthermore, the data show that peak subculturization occurs at 16 and 17 years. In contrast, at 18, the majority of youth desist from gang activity, indicating that powerful forces toward subcultural disintegration operate as adulthood approaches.

Critical points of subculturization differ slightly for group offenders, although the peak age of group and gang subculturization together with the critical point of subcultural desistence are approximately equal. Group offenders are most subculturized at 15 and 16, while exit from the subculture coincides with arrival of adulthood. However, a greater proportion of juveniles 14 years or less incurred police contacts for delinquent group activities (20 percent). Apparently, vulnerability of youth to group subcultural influences appears at a slightly earlier age than susceptibility to gang pressures.

The offender analysis yielded additional evidence indicating the critical points of subculturization. Selective patterns of deviant behavior were similar for gang and group offenders up to and including 13 years; but at 15 a significant divergence in delinquent patterns ensued. Thus, examination of the entire known delinquency histories of gang and group offenders also establishes 14 and 16 as the ages of initial and maximum internecine subculturization. Moreover, the offender data showed that subcultural desistance from both gang and delinquent groups began at 18 years.

Summarizing our findings, we observed that the event and offender analyses yielded evidence, first, that gang and group deviance are different forms of delinquency; second, the gang exerts a powerful influence over the behavior of its participants and, finally, that the ages of subculturization vary for each subculture. The period of susceptibiilty to gang delinquency is shorter, more concentrated, and less diffuse than the span of risk of group delinquency. Apparently, the selective processes operating between the ages of 15 and 17 predisposing youth to engage in internecine delinquency are either absent or of insufficient intensity during earlier years. Contrariwise, the forces of group delinquency appear and are likely to influence youth even during preadolescence (up to age 14). It would be well to consider these observations when formulating a program for prevention and control of gang and group delinquency. The most propitious moment of intervention might indeed coincide with the age immediately prior to initial susceptibility toward a particular variety of delinquency. Preventive action programs concentrating on gang delinquency for instance should be aimed at youth approximately 13 to 14 years of age. Similar attempts to control the more general variety of group delinquency might be more effective with youth in the 10 to 12 years age categories.

6

Factors Influencing the Police
Disposition of Juvenile Offenders

WILLIAM F. HOHENSTEIN

How the police dispose of juveniles caught in the act of delinquency or otherwise brought to police attention is important for a variety of reasons. After it has been ascertained by the juvenile's confession or by adequate circumstantial evidence that he was engaged in a delinquency, should he be dismissed with a warning or turned over to a judicial authority? Extrajudicial dispositions used by the police in juvenile cases are apparently increasing in frequency, judging from national statistics. By avoiding referral to the court, the police often bring parents to the station house to talk over what should be done with the youngster and then return him to his family with stern admonitions or call him to the attention of some welfare agency engaged in preventive work with juveniles and their families. These practices may, of course, be commendable, depending on the skill with which they are employed. The stigmatization of the juvenile as a juvenile court ward is avoided. On the other hand, the practice introduces a disturbing variable in juvenile court intake and disposition statistics that seriously affects the comparability of these statistics in time and space.

In this chapter, we present the results of a study that examines the disposition of juvenile delinquents by the police of Philadelphia, Pennsylvania, during the year 1960. Our data are based on 504 events, representing a 10 percent, fully representative sample of the reported delinquency events occurring that year, and involve juveniles who participated in acts resulting in either injury to persons, loss or damage to property, or both such injury and loss or damage. These are the events which Sellin and Wolfgang used to construct an index of delinquency,[1] and this study examines a detail of the mass of data compiled in the process of developing that index.

The events in question were all brought to the attention of the Juvenile Aid Division of the Philadelphia Police Department. The officers

---

[1] See Thorsten Sellin and Marvin E. Wolfgang, *The Measurement of Delinquency*, (x, 423 pp., New York: John Wiley & Sons, 1964).

of this Division deal with all juvenile suspects. Consequently, they are the persons who decide what should be done with juveniles taken into custody for delinquency, although their decisions may be subject to review by a superior. What factors determine their decisions to arrest juveniles and send them to the detention home, the Youth Study Center, for further processing and perhaps an ultimate court hearing or, instead, to use an alternative which the police call a "remedial" disposition?

The J.A.D. officer's decision is not left to his own discretion. It is:

. . . governed by five criteria, as set forth in training posters, informal talks by Commanding Officers during roll calls, and other forms of indoctrination: (1) the juvenile's previous contacts with the police; (2) the type of offense resulting in his current custody; (3) the attitude of the complainant; (4) the offender's family situation; and (5) potential community resources.[2]

Are the formal criteria mentioned applied or do other factors, such as the age, sex, or race of the delinquent or of his victim, influence the disposition? This study seeks to show what, in practice, are the actual criteria that govern the disposition. By using the data available in the offense reports prepared by the police on the events in question, we shall attempt to develop a predictive typology of dispositions.

METHODOLOGY

To facilitate the understanding of our procedural decisions, we begin with a discussion of the predictive instrument used in the study. The most obvious method of expressing the relationship between a dependent variable, in this case the disposition decision, and numerous independent variables is a mathematical equation. One of the sophisticated methods currently available to the social scientist for constructing such an equation is that of multiple regression. However, because of two assumptions inherently contained in the multiple regression process, it has a rather limited utility in many situations commonly found in the analysis of criminological data. In the first place, it assumes that the population under investigation is homogeneous, that is, that there is no significant difference in the prediction equation for any of the subgroups of the population. It further assumes that the interaction of the predicting variables are additive and linear. These assumptions make the multiple regression technique suitable for discovering and measuring main effects associated with single factors and for specifying certain interactions of factors in a homogeneous population. However, as the number of im-

---

[2] *Ibid.*, p. 95.

portant interactions becomes larger and less specifiable and the population more heterogeneous, the multiple regression equation becomes correspondingly less applicable. Hence, in the current situation, where neither the interaction effects could be specified as being additive and linear nor the population assumed to be homogeneous, an alternate approach to multivariate analysis was employed.

We decided to use a technique originally developed by W. T. Williams and J. M. Lambert of the Botany Department of the University of Southampton,[3] and later adapted for use as a predictive instrument in criminology by Leslie T. Wilkins. The basic problem facing Williams and Lambert was not one of prediction but of classification. Unsatisfied with the methods being used for classifying plots of land into homogenous groups according to species characteristics, they developed a technique which they referred to as association analysis and suggested it as a more efficient way of getting a more accurate picture of the underlying structure of plant groupings. In essence, it is a nonsymmetrical, hierarchical branching process designed to deal with heterogeneity in botanical field data.

Leslie T. Wilkins and Peter MacNaughton-Smith were the first to realize the potential of this analytical technique for use as a predictive tool in criminology. In a paper published in January 1964,[4] they discuss this potential and present a refinement of association analysis aimed at prediction, which they call "Predictive Attribute Analysis (PAA)."

In this technique, the chief concern is with the classification of individuals by the presence or absence of certain attributes shown to be related to the particular phenomenon under investigation. The process divides the sample through a series of binary splits into a set of mutually exclusive and exhaustive subsets. The basic idea in the procedure is the sequential segregation of subgroups, one at a time, so as to arrive at a set of subgroups which will best be able to reduce the error in predicting the dependent variable. At any stage in the branching process, the set of groups developed at that point represents the best possible scheme for predicting the dependent variable in that sample from the information available. If the sample is representative, this is the best scheme for the population.

In order to determine which split to make, the rule is to scan all feasible splits and select the one that most reduces the error variation.

---

[3] W. T. Wiliams and J. M. Lambert, "Multivariate Methods in Plant Ecology, II" *Journal of Ecology*, **48**, 689-710 (1960).

[4] L. T. Wilkins and P. MacNaughton-Smith, "New Prediction and Classification Methods in Criminology," *Journal of Research in Crime and Delinquency*, **1**, 19-32 (January 1964).

The splitting procedure is continued until none of the predicting variables is able to account for a predetermined proportion of the original variance. It is important to point out that the successive divisions will not be of equivalent importance. According to the nature and disposition of the underlying factors, one subdivision may reduce the predictive error enormously; a corresponding division on the other side of the hierarchy may bring about very little reduction. If a variable is used on one of the trunks, and if it shows no actual or potential utility in reducing predictive error in another trunk, then there is clear evidence of a nonlinear interaction effect between that variable and those in the preceding splits. The very existence of nonsymmetry implies interaction.

Once the splitting procedure has stopped, the interpretation of the resulting tree depends upon a number of factors, the chief of which are the characteristics of the final groups themselves. The final groups fall into three with the following chief characteristics:

1. Small groups—those containing too few observations to warrant an attempt to split.

2. Explained groups—over minimum size required for a split but with too little error variation within them to warrant an attempted split.

3. Unexplained groups—those groups with a sufficient number of observations and sufficiently large error variation to justify a split, but no variable in the analysis being successful in reducing the unexplained variation contained within it.

We have noted the character of the sample of delinquent events used in this study. An important assumption made by Sellin and Wolfgang with respect to this sample was that an index of delinquency should be based on delinquent *events* rather than on delinquents and on such events producing injury to a victim and/or loss or damage to property, because they are relatively serious, can be assumed to have a reasonably high degree of reportability and, consequently, fairly represent the universe of such events involving juveniles.

Our second procedural decision was to consider the disposition decision as a function of the delinquent event and not of the delinquent juvenile. Of the 504 events, only three resulted in different dispositions of the juveniles involved. Therefore, it was felt that to consider the disposition decision to be a function of the offender would seriously bias the study in the direction of those events with the greatest number of offenders. However, even though the disposition decision was almost always uniform for each event, it could very well be that information on the offenders' personal backgrounds had much to do with making this decision. For this reason, offender information was noted in each case.

In all, there were fourteen classes of variables considered:

1. Seriousness of the event.
2. Number of victims.
3. Sex of victim.
4. Age of victim.
5. Race of victim.
6. Information on the discovery of the event and the apprehension of the offender.
7. Victim's attitude towards disposition.
8. Number of offenders.
9. Age of offenders.
10. Sex of offenders.
11. Race of offenders.
12. Previous delinquent record of offenders.
13. Victim-offender relationship.
14. Property event information.

CODING

The power of PAA depends upon the accuracy of the coding procedure. In this study, the data recorded and pertaining to the above 14 classifications of variables were broken down into 57 dichotomous situations.

Four different measures of the seriousness of the event were used. The most sensitive was the seriousness scale developed by Sellin and Wolfgang in *The Measurement of Delinquency*. Using scaling procedures, weights were attached to the component parts of a delinquent event and summed to give a single score to the event. This operation had already been carried out on the 501 events finally used in this study,[5] and the only task confronting us was to divide the 501 scores into quartiles for purposes of analysis. The results of this operation were as follows:

Quartile one = seriousness score of one.
Quartile two = seriousness score of two.
Quartile three = seriousness score of three or four.
Quartile four = seriousness score of five or above.

---

[5] We eliminated the three events in which the disposition decisions were not the same for all the delinquents involved.

A second measure of seriousness employed in the study was the grouping of the events.

1. Any event, regardless of legal label, producing bodily injury to at least one of the victims.

2. Any event, regardless of legal label, not producing physical injury to a victim, but involving loss of property through theft.

3. Any event, regardless of legal label, involving only damage to property.

The third measure of seriousness divided the sample of events according to the type of victimization. This process resulted in a fourfold classification:

1. Primary victimization (i.e., cases involving an individual, personal victim).

2. Secondary victimization (i.e., situations in which the victim is a large commercial establishment).

3. Tertiary victimization (i.e., cases in which the victimization extends to the community at large).

4. Mutual participation (i.e., offenses in which there is voluntary participation on the part of both the offender and the other party or parties involved in the event).

The final measure of seriousness was based on the assumption that events in which one or more adults were involved as offenders would be judged as more serious by the police than corresponding events in which no adults were involved. This consideration resulted in a simple dichotomy—presence or absence of an adult. In keeping with the rule of PAA, all of the above measures resulted in mutually exclusive and exhaustive categories.

The variable, "number of victims," was classified into the following three categories:

1. No victim (i.e., no personal victim).
2. One victim.
3. Two or more victims.

A further breakdown of the third category was deemed unnecessary because there were only twenty-one events involving two or more victims.

"Sex of victim" was handled by a simple dichotomy of events in which at least one of the victims was female and those involving no female victim. Because there were only two events with victims of both sexes, there was no justification for adding a third category.

The variable "age of victim" was coded by quartiles:

Quartile one = (0-13) years.

Quartile two = (14-24) years.

Quartile three = (25-42) years.

Quartile four = 43 years and above.

As it was possible to consider the age of only one victim in the coding procedure, the decision was made in those situations involving more than one victim to select the oldest victim for classification on the assumption that his age would be most likely to influence the disposition decision.

The classification of the race of the victims depended on whether the victims were all white or all Negro. The small number of events with victims from both races did not justify the introduction of a mixed category.

The number of offenders involved in the delinquent event was handled by a division into quartiles.

Quartile one = 1 offender.

Quartile two = 2 offenders.

Quartile three = 3 offenders.

Quartile four = 4 or more offenders.

Age and previous record of offenders again involved the problem of having to consider only the characteristics of one of the offenders in multiple offender events. In regard to age, it was decided to use the age of the oldest offender. For a measurement of the previous record, it was decided to consider two factors: (1) the offender with the greatest number of previous offenses and (2) the offender with the greatest number of previous arrests. In almost all cases, these two factors were expressed in the same individual. The number of arrests was introduced in an attempt to get some measure of the seriousness of past offenses. There was not enough information to develop a seriousness score or other sophisticated measure of previous offenses. In all three of these matters—age, previous number of offenses, and arrests—we might have considered using the mean for the offenders in multiple offender events. However, we assumed that the most extreme cases, and not the mean, would be most likely to influence the disposition decision. The following division into quartiles was used:

Age of offender

Quartile one = 11 years or less.

Quartile two = 12 and 13.

Quartile three = 14 and 15.

Quartile four = 16 and 17.

Previous number of offenses
  Quartile one = 0 offenses.
  Quartile two = 1 offense.
  Quartile three = 2-4 offenses.
  Quartile four = 5 or more offenses.

Previous number of arrests
  Quartile one = 0 arrests.
  Quartile two = 1 arrest.
  Quartile three = 2 and 3 arrests.
  Quartile four = 4 or more arrests.

The victim-offender relationship took account of whether the offender was a blood relative of the victim and whether the offender was known to the victim before the event.

A list of variables peculiar to property offenses was also included in the study. These all fell easily into dichotomies.

1. Violence employed.
2. Theft from person.
3. Presence legal at scene of crime.
4. Presence illegal and force employed to gain entry.
5. Presence illegal, no force used.
6. Property recovered in full.
7. Property partially recovered.
8. Victim intimidated by gun, other type of weapon, physically or verbally.

Finally, the attitude of the victim toward the disposition, the situations surrounding the discovery of the act, and the apprehension of the offender were considered. The first posed no coding problems. The last two were handled by asking whether the discovery was made by the police and whether the offender was apprehended by the police.

Before turning to the results of this study, it is necessary to mention the statistical decisions that were made before the analysis was begun. Using Goodman and Kruskal's technique of proportional prediction, it was seen that an attempt to predict the disposition decision of 501 cases with no knowledge of the information detailed above would result, on the average, in 250.21 mistakes.[6] It was also decided to stop the branching process when no variable could account for at least 1 percent of this original error variation.

---

[6] With the variables employed, 64 percent of these mistakes were eliminated.

FINDINGS

An analysis of Fig. 1 reveals that three important factors were involved in determining the disposition decision: (1) the attitude of the victim, (2) the previous record of the offender, and (3) the seriousness of the present event.[7] It will be recalled that these three factors coincide exactly with the first three criteria mentioned by Sellin and Wolfgang in their previously quoted statement.

What is most interesting, however, is the order in which they appear in the typology. Its most striking feature is the primary role played by the attitude of the victim. Regardless of the seriousness of the events or the previous record of the offenders, when victims made statements to the police that they were against prosecution, offenders were "remedialed" in 96 percent of the cases. This fact alone was able to reduce the original error variation by 49 percent. It is also interesting to note that none of the other variables, including a victim's statement in favor of prosecution, was able to reduce the error variation more than 20 percent. All further attempts to split this group of 179 events failed, as none of the other variables was able to account for more than the predetermined 1 percent of the original error variation.

A pertinent fact concerning these 179 events is that more than half of them had a seriousness score greater than one and that, of the seven cases falling into the most serious quartile of seriousness, six were remedialed, thus emphasizing the fact that, regardless of the seriousness of the offense, the victim was likely to be listened to when he wanted the offender released. It is also important to note that the race of the victim had no effect on the degree to which he was listened to by the police. In the events where a white victim made a statement against prosecution, the offender was remedialed 95 percent of the time. When the victim was Negro, the offender was released over 96 percent of the time. The eight events in which the victim's wish was not honored involved five white offenders.

Turning to the 322 events in which no statement was recorded for or against prosecution, the offender was arrested 78 percent of the time. The factor most influential in predicting the disposition of the offenders in these events was the previous number of contacts they had had with the police. When the offender had had more than one previous contact, he was arrested 91 percent of the time; when he had had one or no previous offenses, he was arrested only 53 percent of the time.

---

[7] The prediction typology developed by using "predictive attribute analysis" has a tau B of .69. This can be interpreted to mean that 69 percent of the original error variation has been explained.

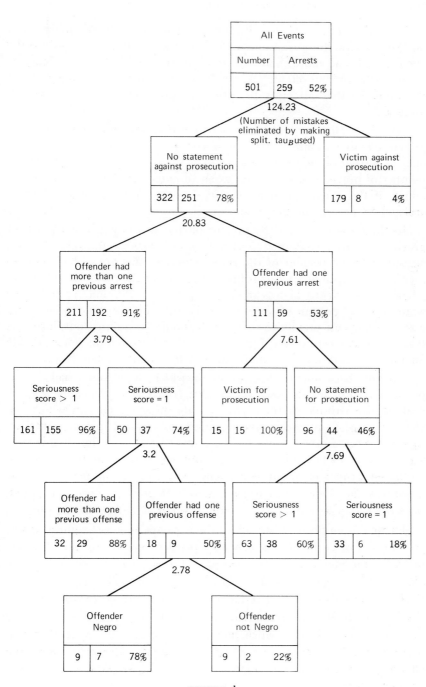

FIGURE 1

The group of 211 cases with longer previous records was further split on the basis of the seriousness of the offense. In the events where the offender had had more than one previous offense and also a seriousness score for the present offense greater than 1, he was arrested 96 percent of the time. Further attempts to split this group of 161 cases were unsuccessful.

When the offender had had more than one previous offense, but the present offense had only a seriousness score of 1, the offender was arrested only 50 percent of the time. This group of 50 cases was further split by the number of previous arrests. Even when the present offense was relatively minor, if the offender had a relatively serious previous record, he was arrested 88 percent of the time.

In those events where the present offense was minor and the list of previous offenses contained only one or no arrests, the offender was arrested only 50 percent of the time. Although this group had only 18 events, it was split again according to the race of the offender. When the offender was a Negro, he was arrested 78 percent of the time; when he was white, only 22 percent of the time. This is the only instance where race was an important predictive variable. It should be pointed out, however, that this result could be a function of other information not available for incorporation into this study, such as the offender's family situation.

Turning back now to those events in which the offender had a good previous record, the dispositions for this group again depended a great deal on the attitude of the victim. In the fifteen events in which the victim wanted to prosecute, the offender was arrested in every instance. In the 96 events in which no such statement was made, the offender was arrested only 46 percent of the time; the deciding factor turned out to be the seriousness of the present offense. When the seriousness score was equal to 1, the offender was arrested in only 18 percent of the cases; when the score was greater than one, he was arrested 60 percent of the time.

Further attempts to split both of these groups ended in failure. It was evident that we still had relatively poor predictive power for the 63 events in which the victim made no statement for or against prosecution, the offender had a good previous record, and the present offense was relatively serious. It appears that factors other than those considered here would have to be known in order to increase the predictive power for this group. Some factors which might prove to be relevant in that connection would be the ability of the Youth Study Center to absorb the offenders, the dress of the offenders, the attitude of the offender to the arresting officer, etc.

SUMMARY

It was pointed out at the beginning of this chapter that the disposition decision made by the J.A.D. officer is important because of the meaning that it has for the child and the community. It has been shown that the attitude of the victim was the primary factor influencing this decision and not the seriousness of the offense or the previous record of the offender, as might be expected. In reference to this point, it was seen, among other things, that an offender with a good previous record and guilty of a minor offense was more likely to be arrested (18 percent) than an offender in an event when the victim refused to prosecute (4 percent), regardless of how serious the present offense was or the length of the offender's previous record of delinquency.

In conclusion, we should mention that no evidence was uncovered to support claims of bias by the police in their disposition of juvenile offenders.

We have demonstrated that the age and sex of both offender and victim were useless in the predictive typology. At no time did these factors come close to splitting any of the groups. The number of offenders in an event also proved to be irrelevant.

BIBLIOGRAPHY

P. MacNaughton-Smith, "The Classification of Individuals by the Possession of Attributes Associated with a Criterion," *Biometrics*, **19**, 364-366 (June 1963).

H. Mannheim and L. T. Wilkins, *Prediction Methods in Relation to Borstal Training* (London: Her Majesty's Stationery Office, 1955).

J. N. Morgan and J. A. Sonquist, "Problems in the Analysis of Survey Data and a Proposal," *Jour. Amer. Statist. Assoc.*, **58**, 415-34 (June 1963).

J. N. Morgan and J. A. Sonquist, "Some Results from a Non-Symmetrical Branching Process that Looks for Interaction Effects," *Proc. Amer. Statist. Assoc.*, 1963, pp. 39-49.

7

Trends in Robbery as Reflected by Different Indexes

ANDRE NORMANDEAU

In the introduction of this volume, reference has been made to the fact that an index of delinquency produced by the system of scoring offensive events as described in *The Measurement of Delinquency* by Sellin and Wolfgang could give results that differ from those arrived at by using the "index crimes" of the Standard Classification of Offenses now employed in, for instance, the *Uniform Crime Reports,* issued by the Federal Bureau of Investigation. In the following pages, this assertion will be illustrated by a comparison of trends of robbery in the city of Philadelphia over a period of seven years, as shown by the two indexes mentioned.

THE PHILADELPHIA STUDY

A 10 percent random sample (1722) of robberies known to the police between January 1, 1960 and December 31, 1966 was studied. Each robbery was given a score of 1 in order to arrive at rates based on the UCR index, and each also scored as a total event to make possible the computation of rates according to the Sellin-Wolfgang method (S-W index) .[1]

Most of the events had S-W scores of 4, 5, or 6, but ranged from some with scores of 2 to a single case with a score of 25, because two armed offenders entered a liquor store, forced three employees and a customer to line up against the wall, took three hundred dollars from the cash register and, before leaving, gun-whipped two of the employees, who were subsequently hospitalized, as well as the customer, who had to be given medical attention.

Figure 1 and Table 1 show the overall trend of rates computed on the principles of the two indexes. According to the S-W index, the rate, as a

---

[1] For a more complete coverage on this robbery study, the reader is referred to A. Normandeau, "Trends and Patterns in Crimes of Robbery," pp. 367, lxxxiii, Ph.D. dissertation, University of Pennsylvania, 1968.

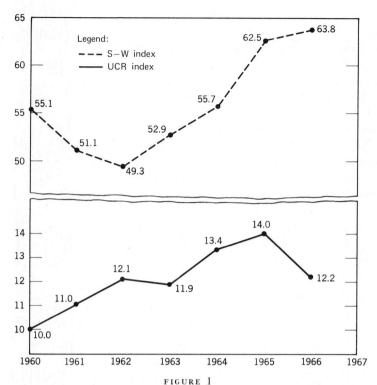

FIGURE 1

Trends in robbery known to police in Philadelphia as shown by the S-W and UCR indexes: 1960 to 1966 (rates per 10,000 total population according to census adjustments).

TABLE 1

Trends in Robbery Known to Police in Philadelphia and Percentages of Increase or Decrease According to the S-W and UCR Indexes: 1960 to 1966

Index	(Rates per 10,000 Total Population According to Census Adjustments)							
	1960	1961	1962	1963	1964	1965	1966	Average
S-W	55.1	51.1	49.3	52.9	55.7	62.5	63.8	55.7
UCR	10.0	11.0	12.1	11.9	13.4	14.0	12.2	12.1

Index	(Percentages of Increase or Decrease from a Year to Another)						
	1960-61	1961-62	1962-63	1963-64	1964-65	1965-66	1960-66
S-W	−7.3	−3.5	+6.8	+5.1	+10.9	+2.0	+13.6
UCR	+9.1	+9.1	−1.7	+11.2	+4.3	−12.3	+18.1
Difference	16.4	12.6	8.5	6.1	6.6	14.3	4.5

measure of the seriousness of harm inflicted in events of robbery, *decreased* from 1960 to 1962 and rose from that year on through 1966, the overall increase from 1960 being 13.6 percent. The UCR index, based on the number of events studied, showed an *increase* from 1960 to 1962, a slight decrease the next year, followed by increases in 1964 and 1965 and a sharp decrease in 1966, the overall increase from 1960 being 18.1 percent. We find ourselves, then, possessing two indexes, which give different and, in part, contradictory interpretations of reality.

The reason for this difference may be found by examining the component elements—injury and theft—of the S-W index.[2] Injury and theft rates show quite dissimilar trends (Figure 2 and Table 2); they are negatively correlated with one another (r:—.90) over the years covered

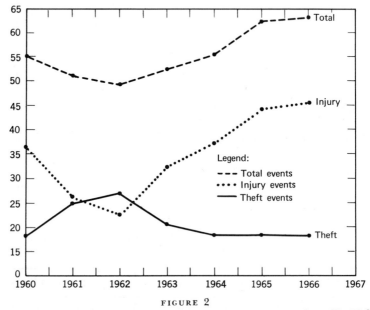

FIGURE 2

Trends in robbery known to police in Philadelphia according to the Sellin-Wolfgang index for total, injury and theft events: 1960 to 1966 (rates per 10,000 total population according to census adjustments).

---

[2] Sellin and Wolfgang relate the injury component to any offense, regardless of its legal title, that produces bodily injury to one or more victims, and where property may or may not be stolen or damaged (*op. cit.*, pp. 154-155), and they relate the theft component to any offense, regardless of its legal title, that does not produce physical injury to the victim but which involves the loss of property through theft, and where the property stolen may or may not be damaged (*op. cit.*, p. 154). The authors also suggest a damage component which excludes the two others. However, because our data showed a very small amount of damage, we have included the cases in this category with theft.

TABLE 2

Trends in Robbery Known to Police in Philadelphia According to the S-W Index for Total, Injury and Theft Events: 1960 to 1966

Elements	(Rates per 10,000 Total Population According to Census Adjustments)							
	1960	1961	1962	1963	1964	1965	1966	Average
Injury	36.8	26.0	22.3	32.4	37.2	44.1	45.6	34.9
Theft	18.3	25.1	27.0	20.5	18.5	18.4	18.2	20.8
Total	55.1	51.1	49.3	52.9	55.7	62.5	63.8	55.7
Injury percent of total	66.6	50.9	45.2	61.2	66.8	70.6	71.5	62.7

by the study. In fact, while injury rates more or less parallel the total rates (r:.96), theft rates are negatively related to them (r:—.78). The injury component usually dominates the total because the scores of seriousness for bodily injury are higher than the scores for the bulk of the money categories associated with theft. If the injury elements are qualitatively more important in certain years, they will increase the total rates of seriousness in such a disproportionate way that even decreases, for example, in the UCR *number* of robberies will not become apparent because the events, though less numerous, are of a more serious nature. This is what happened in 1963 and 1966. The contrary was true in 1961 and 1962. Cases of injury involving treatment and hospitalization have, as a matter of fact, decreased and increased according to similar decreases or increases in total rates, while the number of thefts in the different money categories has remained relatively stable over the years.[3]

DELINQUENCY PER SE

Data computed individually for robbery events cleared by the arrest of juveniles are not given in detail here,[4] but we may say that they indicate, over time, patterns of increases or decreases strictly similar to the rates for all events, cleared and uncleared (as seen in the preceding section). It must be kept in mind that, because only about 40 percent of robberies in Philadelphia are cleared by arrest and only about 35 percent

[3] The specific data about these items are given in Normandeau, *op. cit.*, pp. 109-110.
[4] See Normandeau, *op. cit.*, pp. 104-106.

of these cleared offenses are cleared by the arrest of juveniles, juvenile rates per se contribute only to about 10 to 15 percent of the total rates. In any event, what is important is the fact that the specific juvenile rates, as assessed by the S-W index and the UCR index, respectively, also show dissimilar trend profiles and that the breakdown of the S-W index into injury and theft elements can explain this differentiation too.

SERIOUSNESS PER EVENT AND OFFENDER

Table 3, which presents data derived from the S-W index,[5] gives an even clearer picture of this increase of seriousness by event from 1962 to 1966 (as well as the prior decrease from 1960 to 1962) and of the predominant impact of the injury component. It also shows similar patterns when we are talking of average seriousness per offender.

It is important to note that seriousness per juvenile event or juvenile offender is consistently greater (although not significantly so) than for all robbery events taken together. It may be explained by the fact that the number of offenders per event is greater for juvenile events (see Table 3 also) and that the larger the group of offenders facing a victim, the greater the probability that injurious violence will take place (as was confirmed further on in the study). This finding about juveniles is important because it contradicts the hypothesis often made about the so called "nasty but not serious" juvenile behavior in crimes of robbery.[6]

CONCLUSION

The differential trend profiles of the S-W index and the UCR index can thus be understood by the variation within the components of robbery as given to us by the S-W index, which takes into account both the quality and the quantity of crime. The UCR index has, obviously, an important disadvantage on this count and, thus, seems less accurate in its

---

[5] The specific formulas and their explanations corresponding to the different types of indexes given in Table 3 are developed in Normandeau, *op. cit.*, pp. 97-99.

[6] This hypothesis, with reference to robbery, was made in particular by R. H. Beattie, "A System of Integrated Criminal Statistics," *Criminologica*, 5, 12-19 (1967); N. S. Winnet, T. Sellin, and N. Teeters, in the *Annual Report, 1956*, Crime Prevention Association of Philadelphia, pp. 1, 8, and 11; and M. E. Wolfgang, "The Culture of Youth," in *Task Force Report: Juvenile Delinquency and Youth Crime*, U.S. President's Commission on Law Enforcement and the Administration of Justice (Washington, D.C.: U. S. Government Printing Office, 1967), pp. 145-154, at p. 150.

TABLE 3

Indexes of Seriousness per Event and Offender for Crimes of Robbery in Philadelphia: 1960 to 1966. Philadelphia Sample.

Type of Index		1960	1961	1962	1963	1964	1965	1966	Average
Seriousness per event (for all events)	Injury	4.80	4.46	4.51	4.88	4.95	5.01	5.51	4.87
	Theft	4.01	3.31	3.10	3.55	3.68	3.82	3.01	3.50
	Total	4.50	4.08	4.03	4.46	4.51	4.60	4.81	4.42
Seriousness per *juvenile* event	Injury	5.07	4.55	4.50	5.02	5.00	5.33	5.84	5.04
	Theft	3.75	3.20	3.11	4.03	3.99	4.19	3.02	3.61
	Total	4.62	4.19	4.14	4.60	4.59	4.75	4.95	4.55
Seriousness per offender (for all offenders)	Injury	2.24	2.04	2.04	2.19	2.40	2.46	2.70	2.30
	Theft	2.03	1.75	1.71	1.79	1.96	1.99	1.81	1.86
	Total	2.15	1.91	1.90	2.04	2.21	2.28	2.41	2.12
Seriousness per *juvenile* offender	Injury	2.31	2.21	2.32	2.38	2.69	2.76	3.01	2.53
	Theft	2.10	1.71	1.59	1.68	2.02	1.91	2.12	1.88
	Total	2.24	2.04	2.01	2.16	2.40	2.44	2.71	2.29
Average offender seriousness (for all events)	Injury	5.42	5.03	5.00	5.30	5.44	5.59	5.78	5.37
	Theft	4.07	4.14	4.19	4.31	4.01	4.00	3.61	4.05
	Total	4.90	4.71	4.70	4.88	4.92	4.99	5.21	4.90
Average *juvenile* offender seriousness	Injury	5.71	5.31	5.35	5.43	5.51	5.70	5.99	5.57
	Theft	3.92	4.03	3.88	4.49	4.31	4.15	4.70	4.21
	Total	5.10	4.95	4.95	5.07	5.19	5.31	5.60	5.17

TABLE 3

Indexes of Seriousness per Event and Offender for Crimes of Robbery in Philadelphia: 1960 to 1966. Philadelphia Sample.

Type of Index		1960	1961	1962	1963	1964	1965	1966	Average
Average seriousness (for all events)	Injury	.0051	.0048	.0044	.0050	.0055	.0060	.0065	.0053
	Theft	.0020	.0014	.0017	.0019	.0019	.0019	.0020	.0018
	Total	.0071	.0062	.0061	.0069	.0074	.0079	.0085	.0072
Average juvenile seriousness	Injury	.0067	.0057	.0055	.0062	.0072	.0075	.0091	.0068
	Theft	.0021	.0018	.0019	.0023	.0019	.0022	.0018	.0020
	Total	.0088	.0075	.0074	.0085	.0091	.0097	.0109	.0088
Offenders per event (for all events)	Injury	1.50	1.49	1.55	1.15	1.26	1.48	1.29	1.39
	Theft	1.22	1.27	1.17	1.01	1.05	1.19	1.13	1.14
	Total	1.35	1.39	1.30	1.07	1.16	1.34	1.21	1.26
Juvenile offenders per event	Injury	2.21	2.30	2.08	1.81	1.88	1.99	1.90	2.02
	Theft	1.64	1.51	1.39	1.11	1.23	1.42	1.29	1.37
	Total	1.95	1.98	1.75	1.51	1.60	1.74	1.65	1.74
Offender's in average offender's event (for all events)	Injury	2.47	2.59	2.35	2.11	2.22	2.42	2.18	2.37
	Injury	2.01	2.02	1.98	1.55	1.64	1.91	1.89	1.91
	Total	2.28	2.34	2.19	1.90	1.99	2.21	2.08	2.18
Offender's in average juvenile offender's event	Injury	3.61	3.54	3.21	3.04	3.18	3.20	3.15	3.28
	Theft	2.93	3.05	2.69	2.48	2.62	2.77	2.70	2.75
	Total	3.30	3.35	3.05	2.80	2.94	3.03	2.98	3.06

assessment of the crime trends or, at least, within the context of the present study, of the trends in robbery.

The UCR's sytem, surely, serves practical purposes for the law enforcement agencies, and we are *not* proposing its *replacement* by the new Sellin-Wolfgang system. However, the UCR's scheme suffers severe deficiencies in regard to its capabilities to shed light on the "real" trends in criminality in this country, and we think that the Sellin-Wolfgang scheme should be used, in this perspective, as a valid *supplement* to the official one now prevalent.

Index